The Human Tree

By Benjamin Minch

Cover Designed by Noa Wilding

Edited in Part by Phoebe Wicks

To all those whom have mentored me
thus far…

TABLE OF CONTENTS

1

THE TREE OF LIFE

I don't really know why the human race has an obsession with trees. Throughout history, trees have always had a sort of spirituality to them; a deeper meaning than pure physicality. Starting with the Garden of Eden itself, the tree of life and the tree of the knowledge of good and evil are present. In Buddhism, the Bodhi tree holds a special significance as the spot in which Siddhartha sat when reaching enlightenment. In Hinduism, the Peepal tree is sacred for its supposed use in lighting the first sacred fire through which the gods granted knowledge to humanity. In modern times, the family tree and the evolutionary tree of life have been images that people have become quite fond of.

We fantasize over trees and rightly so. Ever since reading Peter Wohlleben's *The Hidden Life of Trees* [1], trees have been an obsession of mine. Certain tree species can share nutrients with other trees through fungal root growths or interconnected roots. Trees can recognize roots of other trees of the same species and specifically send nutrients to family members to boost survivability. Acacia trees give off a warning gas to their neighbors in order to tell them to pump toxins into their leaves when aphids attack. Other species can release pheromones to attract specific predators to the tree to eat specific pests such as bark beetles. Trees can cooperate to release pollen and seeds at the same time to increase the chance of them landing in a fertile area. Mother trees nurse infant trees through root networks. Trees can tell time: knowing how long days are and how many consecutive warm days have passed as a way to help them know when to drop their leaves. Trees can do many more amazing things, but this book isn't concerned as much at what trees can do. It is what they symbolize that is of importance in this book.

Growing a tree is even harder work than studying them. All well-versed gardeners know this. Soil is a vastly important part of healthy tree growth as each tree needs its own specific soil conditions to thrive. Soil can have a range of pH, nitrogen or phosphorus levels, or even different parasites.-Planting a tree in the wrong type of soil could even kill the tree. The most complicated part of soil though is that it is hard to pinpoint what the actual problem is. If a tree is looking sick, bad soil is one of the last thoughts that come to mind. The usual culprits are lack of water, sunlight, or space. It is much harder to diagnose a soil problem and even more so a problem beneath the soil that we cannot see. This idea will be explored in this book as we look at how the soils of history have affected the fruit of the human tree.

If you were expecting biology, sorry to disappoint. This book will be mostly focused on history, using a giant metaphor of the human race as a tree. The "soils" in this case represent the different ideologies and thought patterns that governed and influenced the "tree" or humanity during each given historical era. Although no historian myself, I have researched this book extensively and plan to share my insights into the history of the human race. Disclaimer: this book will only cover Western history, as I have grown up in the West and received a Western education, therefore knowing the most about its history.

One trap that we can fall into when we think about history is assuming that our ways of thinking and insight in our current historical period is somehow superior to every civilization in the past. Some may say that historical ideas are outdated, and therefore we should focus on our present-day problems and ideologies, but this is in fact not the most helpful way to look at the world. In his famous defense of reading old books C.S. Lewis, a famous 20th-century theologian, regurgitated the quote from *On the Incarnation*, "None of us can fully escape this blindness, but we shall certainly increase it, and weaken our guard against it, if we read only modern books" [2]. We may think that our current cultural framework is infallible and the current way of life and thinking about problems is the supreme way, but this is simply not the case. This same thought pattern was shared by every other civilization throughout history: by great leaders such as Alexander the Great, Abraham Lincoln, and Winston Churchill, and by terrible leaders such as Adolf Hitler, Genghis Khan, and Joseph Stalin. Everybody's way of thinking cannot be perfect, and this is why we need history to examine our blindness in thinking. After all, the Western mindset was formed out of a series of historical events, so it would follow that it is beneficial to learn from the founders of our minds about the potential dangers that could come from this mindset.

Another trap we fall into when looking at history is assuming that the human race has progressed in a straight line from bad to better and that where we are now is the best we have ever been in human history. This thought pattern is enforced by popular evolutionary thinking and false application of this evolutionary thinking to culture. According to Darwin's theory of evolution, species gradually progressed from simple to more complex, climaxing with humankind. This mindset applied to culture is known as Social Darwinism, and has had negative implications wherever it has been applied. Social Darwinism, rooted in the idea that the human race is progressing from good to great, has been the driving ideology behind Hitler's Germany, Stalin's Russia, the Americanization of the Native Americans, and imperialism of other nations. If you believe that the ultimate goal of modern society is to evolve into a better version of itself, then you can justify extreme measures such as eugenics, ethnic cleansing, and indoctrination. Darwin himself was against the unintended implications of his theory, as he himself wasn't a social Darwinist [3]. History and the human race do not progress slowly in a straight line from bad to better as the Social Darwinist wants you to believe. The high points of the renaissance were countered by the low points of the dark ages. The high morality and rationality of the enlightenment was countered by the nihilism and helplessness of the World Wars. In every era and time period, there are good things and bad things and we can learn from them both.

I guarantee that you could find a good counterexample to every event I point out in this book. This task, however, would be missing the very point. This book isn't a huge compilation of historical critique and exposition; it is a narrative. I am not concerned with every little detail throughout history, I am more concerned with trends and cycles. It may jostle some edges, and you may not agree with certain parts of this book, but that is also not my goal. If it were then I'd have to lie about so much of history to be likable. This I am not willing to do.

This short book serves to be a giant extended metaphor for the human race. Using the image of the tree and its soil, we will closely examine the past 2000 or so years of human history and what made each age both great and horrific. We will see the great fruit of the soil of religion, secularism, technology, love and peace, capitalism, postmodernism, and our current Western soil. But we will also look at the bad fruit as you can always learn from history. If you are the type of person that has killed one too many plants while gardening, then you'll relate with this metaphor greatly. You will know the pain of planting a tree just to have it die a few months later without seemingly having done anything wrong. You will have experienced the constant uprooting and replanting of your prized lavender bush into different types of soil until it survives just long enough to bloom flowers. But if you haven't experienced the ups and downs of gardening, that is okay too. This book is meant to enlighten us all to the deep roots of the human race; roots that cut through culture, geography, ethnicity, politics, social status, and skin color. These are the very roots of the human tree, now let's go on a journey through time.

2

THE SOIL OF RELIGION

Jumping out of our time machine in the year 312 CE, Europe was a completely different landscape than today. This is to be expected because 1700 years has surely done a lot to upgrade technology, population, and cities. Physical things weren't the only difference in this early fourth-century world, however. The century was defined by one major event, one that would change the European landscape for the next 1000 years. This event became known as the Constantine shift and marked a huge shift in thought towards favoring Christianity and the Church. Before this, persecution of Christians was rampant across the Roman Empire. Martyrs were thrown into the colosseum to fight lions, used as human candlesticks, and crucified, all for their claims to be Christian. Before 312 CE, being a Christian meant being an outsider and the task of following Christ usually ended in death for his sake. In fact, as of 303 CE Christians were still being persecuted as the Roman emperor Diocletian launched the most brutal round of persecution towards Christians that they had ever experienced. Around 312 CE, this began to change with the acceptance of Christianity by Constantine, the next emperor of Rome. He passed the Edict of Milan in 313 CE which legalized Christianity and other religions in the Roman empire. Christianity had turned from being a minority persecuted group to becoming popular among much of the nation. The conditions in Rome made it almost favorable to be a Christian because of legislation that gave the Church certain benefits that the rest of society such as financial support and increased access to education. Constantinople, the then capital of Rome, now contained Christian churches alongside its pagan temples. Christians were given money by the emperor and land to build new churches. In 380 CE, Christianity was made the state religion of the Roman Empire. It wasn't very difficult to be a Christian in the age of religion and by the 16th century, their numbers were massive across Europe.

This large shift in thought towards religion marks the beginning of the planting of the human race in the soil of religion. Christianity became a popular phenomenon and there was a tight interlocking between Church and state that would become evident in the later years of the age of religion. Before 300 CE, Christians only made up 10% or less of the Roman Empire, but in 350 CE, they had come to make up 56.5% according to ancient sociologist Rodney Stark in *The Rise of Christianity* [1]. It was growing at a rate of nearly 40% a decade. With the rising of tight connections between the teachings of the Bible and the teachings of the state, many good fruits came out of the human tree at this time.

The Good Fruits

When we discuss the good fruits of the human tree in the soil of religion, we run into a problem: What constitutes a good fruit? Many events occurred in this age that the vast majority of Christians today would call "good", but other secular sources wouldn't render as "good" such as the reformation and the rise of religious saints such as Augustine of Hippo and Thomas Aquinas. These events were very good for the world of Christianity, but the modern skeptic isn't going to care a rat's tail about the reformation, or these saints of old because they have no effect on his current life. Therefore, in order to be constituted a good fruit, it must be considered "good" by all types of people. Whether you are a believer in Jesus Christ, Buddha, or no higher being at all, you should be able to agree that these fruits that came out of the soil of religion were in fact good [2].

The Intellectualization of Europe

One of the greatest fruits to come from the age of religion was the intellectualization of Europe and the West. During this time, the first university was built in 1088, the University of Bologna in Italy. Many others followed such as Oxford, Cambridge, and Salamanca in Spain. These universities were devoted to teaching people about theology, law, and medicine and many required you to be a Christian to study there. Harvard was founded during this period in 1636 with the initial purpose to train clergy and by the end of the 17th century, 106 of the 108 colleges in America were founded by Christians. The Christian purpose in universities is apparent in a reading of the student rulebook from Harvard during the 1600s

"Let every Student be plainly instructed, and earnestly pressed to consider well, the main end of his life and studies is, to know God and Jesus Christ which is eternal life (John 17:3) and therefore to lay Christ in the bottom, as the only foundation of all sound knowledge and Learning. And seeing the Lord only giveth wisdom, let everyone seriously set himself by prayer in secret to seek it of him (Prov. 2:3)." [3]

The rise of the university is one of the great successes of human history, as universities today advance our understanding of the world and each other. The modern university has very Christian roots as these Universities were established by Christians for the sake of learning more about the world God created. The scholastic movement, of which Thomas Aquinas was a part of, brought the world of reason and education into the church and valued learning everything they could get their hands on. They wanted to seek out this truth which they knew existed because they worshiped a God who made all truth. To the early believers, religion and education went hand in hand and many of the most prominent religious figures of the time such as Martin Luther, Augustine of Hippo, and Thomas Aquinas pursued education very seriously. Luther celebrated education and the arts precisely because he believed in God, not despite it. In a preface for *Walter's Hymn Book*, he makes this point.

"I do not hold the opinion that all the arts are to be completely discarded through the Gospel, as some super-spiritual people would have it; but I would like to see all arts, especially music, placed in the service of Him who has given and created them." [4]

Accompanying the rise of the university and the education of Europe came the Scientific Revolution. A period of immense scientific progress that we owe much of our modern society to, the Scientific Revolution was one of the good fruits of the religious soil. Many famous inventions and discoveries came out of this period such as the discovery of gravity, the development of the telescope, and the structure of the heart. This was one of the most significant events of human history and sociologists such as the Hungarian Joseph Ben-David argue that it completely changed our world of thought.

"Rapid accumulation of knowledge, which has characterized the development of science since the 17th century, had never occurred before that time. The new kind of scientific activity emerged only in a few countries of Western Europe, and it was restricted to that small area for about two hundred years." [5]

Many of the greatest minds that were behind the Scientific Revolution, Isaac Newton, Johannes Kepler, Nicolaus Copernicus, Galileo Galilei, René Descartes, and many others were devout Christians in addition to being excellent astronomers, philosophers, physicists, and mathematicians. Their belief in God as the source of all truth and creator of the universe propelled them into studying it further. Descartes expresses this sentiment when he makes the statement "God alone is the author of all the motions in the world.". Similarly, Sir Robert Boyle, one of the founders of modern chemistry, expresses the same motivation for his research stating that "Nature is nothing else but God acting according to certain laws he fixed". Isaac Newton himself spent much more time studying theology than science and wrote more than 2 million words on religion in his lifetime. Kepler looked at the cosmos through the telescope and proclaimed that "God ever geometrizes!". The scientific revolution was undoubtedly Christian at its roots and came as one of the great fruits of the soil of religion. As historian Peter Harrison puts it in his book *The Territories of Science and Religion*:

"Historians of science have long known that religious factors played a significantly positive role in the emergence and persistence of modern science in the West. Not only were many of the key figures in the rise of science individuals with sincere religious commitments, but the new approaches to nature that they pioneered were underpinned in various ways by religious assumptions. ... Yet, many of the leading figures in the scientific revolution imagined themselves to be champions of a science that was more compatible with Christianity than the medieval ideas about the natural world that they replaced." [6]

Until the French Revolution, the Catholic Church was the leading sponsor of scientific research, and until Darwin, the large majority of scientists were professing Christians. Starting in the Middle Ages, the Church paid for priests, monks, and friars to study at the universities. The soil of religion produced the great fruit of education on the human tree, one that still holds a very high value in today's Western world.

The Renaissance

While the intellectualization of Europe was transforming the intellectual sphere, the renaissance was transforming the cultural sphere of this time. The renaissance refers to the period between the 14th and 17th centuries in which there was a fervent "rebirth" in European art, politics, and culture. This period gave us the great basilicas and cathedrals of Rome, the great frescoes and murals such as the Last supper and the ceiling of the Sistine Chapel, and many famous statues such as Michelangelo's David. The renaissance began in Florence Italy because of the wealthiness and ability to support the arts. One of the earliest supporters of the movement was the famous Medici family, patronizing many famous artists to kickstart the movement. It quickly spread beyond Florence and became a Europe-wide phenomenon.

Many of the most well-known historical figures came out of this period such as Leonardo da Vinci, Michelangelo, Donatello, Raphael, Dante, Erasmus, Hobbes, William Shakespeare, and Niccolo Machiavelli. All of these artists, philosophers, and sculptors combined their fields of expertise to create a time of high art and thought. For example, da Vinci incorporated many scientific findings into his art such as his painting of the anatomical man. Architects worked with mathematicians to create the perfect domes for new buildings and many artworks portrayed new natural findings. This was a time of unprecedented art and innovation and many of the artists and paintings remain precious even today.

There is little doubt that the renaissance, like the scientific revolution, was a highly religious undertaking. Coming from the soil of religion, many of the patrons of the arts were high up nobility in the Catholic Church or even the pope himself. Many of the frescoes painted depicted religious events or stories such as The Last Supper by da Vinci or the Creation of Man by Michelangelo. Renaissance artists were driven by their love for beauty, an experience they connected intimately with God's creative power. The biographer of Michelangelo, Ascanio Condivi, wrote that "Michelangelo loved not only human beauty but universally every beautiful thing" [7]. Their love for beauty naturally followed from their love of God as the creator and ultimate source of beauty. Beauty was out there for them to discover, create, and appreciate. Many of the renaissance artists had a high view of the human body, both male and female, and celebrated the beauty of God's created body (although this usually meant the paintings are explicit to young modern eyes).

The renaissance was a time of high art, culture, politics, and science. Following the depravity of the Middle ages and Black Death, it provided stability and pushing of all the boundaries of the modern culture at the time. Never before (or since) had there been such a coming together of art, science, and philosophy. The seeds of the modern world were sown and grown in the Renaissance. From circumnavigating the world to the discovery of the solar system, from the beauty of Michelangelo's David to the perfection of Leonardo's Mona Lisa, from the genius of Shakespeare to the daring of Luther and Erasmus, and via breathtaking advances in science and mathematics, man achieved new heights in this tumultuous period. This was a very good fruit of the religious soil.

The Bad Fruits

While the age of religion bolstered both the sciences and the arts, all was not perfect in this age of innovation and deep religiosity. You would think that with the vast majority of Europe following the same God, things would be great, and no bad fruit could be produced, but unfortunately, this was not the case. Many of the good fruits of the soil of religion also inevitably lead to bad fruits of application. Scientific advances lead to the invention of gunpowder and other weapons of mass destruction, the quest for knowledge led to some of the most brutal religious wars, and the improved navigational capabilities lead to the brutalization of many Native Americans in the

New World. Although a time of great progress for those inside the nobility or intellectual realm, this was a time of war, brutalization, and abuse for those outside of these spheres.

Religious Wars

One of the greatest perils of the soil of religion was the immense number and brutality of religious wars. The most prominent of these was the Crusades, which lasted from 1096 to 1271 with the primary goal of reclaiming the Holy land of Jerusalem from Islamic control. These wars were initiated, supported, and directed by the church at the time. David Hume, an enlightenment thinker, described the Crusades as "the most signal and durable monument of human folly that has yet appeared in any age or any nation". Of course, Hume had not lived through Hitler's Germany or Stalin's Russia, but it was still a very telling claim that he made about the horrors of the religious wars.

The Crusades are almost a direct expression of the authority that the papacy held in the Middle ages. The fact that the church could assemble an army of around 30,000 men is unheard-of today, although some may say that the army has shifted to a political force rather than a physical one. Many of the Crusaders, as they were called, firmly believed that violence for the faith earned them a heavenly reward, not too dissimilar from modern terrorists. St Bernard of Clairvaux, a French abbot at the time of the first Crusades, wrote:

"Of mighty soldier, oh man of war, you now have something to fight for. If you win it will be glorious. If you die fighting for Jerusalem, you will win a place in heaven".

On top of the heavenly reward offered, the Crusaders were also promised the forgiveness of their sins for partaking in this battle. At the time the people genuinely thought that the pope had the ability to do this and so this cleansed their conscious of having to kill people during the wars. The Crusades were justified using misinterpreted warfare metaphors of the New Testament as passages such as Matthew 16:24:

"Then Jesus said to his disciples, "Whoever wants to be my disciple must deny themselves and take up their cross and follow me." "

They waved the banners of justice, "Christianization" and the will of God, all while causing injustice, and destroying precious image-bearers of God in the process. The call of "Christianization" was really just a religious gloss to ethnic cleansing. During this time between 1 and 3 million people were killed and Muslims, as well as Jews, were indiscriminately murdered, and their places of worship were burned to the ground all in the name God. Many sermons preached during this time purported to manipulate public support for the wars and to fire up support for their efforts. There was even a distinctive preaching formula or method developed at this time that combined the use of justification of the Crusades from scripture and a moral degrading of the "infidels" they were to destroy.

The Christians are not all to blame for the Crusades though, as history is never as simple as the books make it out to be. The causes and purpose for the Crusades are very complex and nuanced topics of which there is much debate and discussion around. In some cases, the Christians were perfectly justified in defending their land against the foreign invaders, as the "infidels" threatened to destroy their known world. I do, however, think that they went too far in their pursuits.

This point is made in looking at the brutality of the Crusades, which can be summed up in many small stories relating to men on the front lines of the wars. According to one Christian Englishman, "Death is sweet when the victor lies encircled by impious people he has slain with his victorious right hand". The bloodshed in the Crusades was immense and according to one of the most contemporary accounts, *Gesta Francorum*, "the slaughter was so great that our men waded in blood up to their ankles" [8]. The methods of killing were even more brutal. Before the sacking of one of the Islamic towns of Lastours, Simon de Montfort, one of the crusaders, took prisoners and had their eyes gouged out as well as their noses and ears cut off. The King of France at the time turned a blind eye to this violence and in a later account of his actions, historian Alistair Horne recounts that he "readily accepted the spoils to his exchequer". Even non-Christians living in Europe did not escape the violence of the Crusades. Many were deemed heretics and "threats to the mission" and were assassinated.

The Crusades, while being the most brutal and well-documented of the religious wars, was not the only one that took place during this time. The Thirty Years War, called such because it lasted 30 years from 1618 to 1648, was one of the most destructive conflicts in human history with an estimated death toll of 8 million. This war started because of religious differences between the Roman Catholic Church and protestants, as the Catholics forced citizens of the Holy Roman Empire (now Germany) to become Catholic. This assault on religious freedom was too much for the protestants to be passive and thus, the Thirty Years War began. The war itself was the most damaging event in Europe at the time, as the effects of the war were seen throughout the continent. Famine was widespread because of the destruction of many farms during the war and diseases such as Typhoid were also prevalent because of the poor conditions of the war-torn villages. [9]

Many other religious wars could be named here such as the peasant's revolt during the reformation, the French wars of religion, the Hussite Wars, the War of the Three Henrys, and the nine-year war, but I will save you the details. Expanding on the brutalities of all of these wars would be gratuitous as the message is already across there were many abuses of religion to oppress people and to take land from enemies. Millions of deaths during this time owe their cause to the banner of religion and Christianization of Europe, something antithetical to the very Christian message. It is easy to see how this is a bad fruit produced from the human tree in the soil of religion.

The Social Abuses of the Church

With the tight union between Church and State that arose during the period of religious soil, there was inevitably a power imbalance. The church was heavily involved in the business of gaining more wealth and power to have more influence over its citizens. The Church at the time was even above the kings, as often the pope was the one to confirm kings and give them the divine right to rule

the people. The Church also had a monopoly on knowledge, especially knowledge of the scriptures. With the Bible only being in Latin at the time, very few people could actually read it and even if they could read Latin, the only Bibles were often locked up and reserved for only the most religious of people. With nobody being able to gain knowledge apart from the pope, the pope became an authoritarian ruler and the source of all truth.
With this seemingly unlimited power, the Church was a breeding ground for corruption. Many religious positions were open to the highest bidder; a process known as Simony. This led to many higher-ups in the church having little grasp of true Christianity so they would say conflicting things that often had little to do with the Bible.

The church also had developed a highly profitable relic collection. Many artifacts that are of interest to the history of Christianity such as a thorn off of Jesus's crown, a wood fiber from the cross, or the garments of Saint Paul, were collected by high-up members of the church. The Roman Catholic Church held that owning or even gazing upon these relics could grant you or someone you love that is now dead, fewer years in purgatory, their version of a waiting room in the afterlife. Many Christians at the time would make long pilgrimages and pay large sums of money just to see the relics, which often were fakes.

Along with the practice of relics came the most infamous source of corruption, indulgences. Indulgences were pieces of paper that one could buy in order to reduce their time spent in purgatory and forgive sins, much like the relics. These were sold by the Church to raise funds for the building of St. Peter's Basilica, and they were bought up by the masses. Who wouldn't want to spend earthly money on heavenly blessing? There were even special "plenary indulgences" which could grant you complete pardon from your sins at a higher price. This greatly divided society among socioeconomic lines, as many who were in poverty, felt pressured to purchase indulgences over feeding their family. The most famous seller of indulgences was Johann Tetzel, who was commissioned by the pope to raise money for the Basilica. He is famous for his selling phrase of "When a penny in the coffer rings, A soul from Purgatory springs". He was a widespread success and owes his success largely to the fear that many people had about purgatory and suffering. What the pope preached in the pulpit was firmly linked to the sale of indulgences and a vicious cycle had begun in order to milk the people of their money. This system of indulgences and monetization of grace and forgiveness was one of the main concerns of Martin Luther, a prominent protestant reformer, in his 95 theses he posted on the Wittenberg chapel.

"Why does not the pope liberate everyone from purgatory for the sake of love (the holiest thing) and because of the supreme necessity of their souls? This would be morally the best of reasons. Meanwhile, he redeems innumerable souls for money, a most perishable thing, with which to build St. Peter's church, a very minor purpose." [10]

With this seemingly unlimited power, the Roman Catholic Church during the time of religious soil had turned into a money-making machine. The common person was forced into this system because they knew no better as literacy was rare for this period. This abuse of power is most definitely a bad fruit from the human tree, and it would take a full-scale reformation in order to set the church back on its feet and restore the key doctrines of Christianity.

Unfortunately, one of the greatest fruits of the religious soil turned into one of the worst fruits of the time. With the onset of the Scientific Revolution, improvements in ocean navigation methods led to the ability to travel around the world. Christopher Columbus was one of the most popular navigators as he sailed to the New World in 1492, but others soon followed such as Vasco de Gama, Sir Francis Drake, and Ferdinand Magellan. The discovery that these new territories were not uninhabited, led to the beginning of the abuse of the Native American populations and the eventual wiping out of many tribes and cultures. Upon arriving in the New World, Christopher Columbus wrote back to England "These people are very unskilled in arms... with 50 men they could all be subjected and made to do all that one wished". This would be the mindset of the vast majority of New World conquerors of the time, even the Christian ones.

The Native American cultures present in the New World practiced a wide variety of spiritual customs and religious ceremonies which varied greatly between tribe and people. According to a professional on Native American culture, "Dances and religious ceremonies often centered on The Great Spirit, believed by many Native Americans to be the [faceless] creator of life or the supreme being . . . Festivals and ceremonies included chanting, singing, and dancing. The clothing worn by both males and females of the tribes were extraordinarily detailed" [11]. Tragically, the Native Americans' free exercise of peaceful religious practices and beliefs did not last forever. The arrival of conquerors and colonizers with weapons in each hand, a gun in their right, and a bible in their left would mean the widespread oppression, persecution, and condemnation of the spiritual beliefs and practices that were so central to the lives of the Native Americans.

From early on in the exploration of the New World, Catholicism and Protestantism emerged as major influences. Christopher Columbus, after his first encounter with the Native People, wrote:

"I gave them many beautiful things in order to win their affection, and that they might become Christians … they are very ready for conversion to the holy faith in Christ …

[they] are so naïve and so free with their possession that no one who has not witnessed them would believe it" [12]

He earnestly believed and freely used religious reasoning to justify his selfish ambitions in the New World saying that "the eternal God, our Lord, gives victory to those who follow His way over apparent impossibilities". Colonizers enslaved Native Americans under the decree of the pope at the time, Pope Nicholas V, simply because they were enemies to Christ, not because they were threatening or enemies of war. These Native Americans became conscripted laborers, forced into the mines and the fields as slaves and encomenderos, the property of the Spanish conquistador who had been granted their land. Many plagues were also brought upon the Native Americans by the Europeans such as smallpox, which wiped out millions of Native peoples. One of the major colony leaders, John Winthrop, however, actually saw the plagues as gain, referring to the smallpox epidemics as "the means by which 'God hath . . . cleared our title to this place,' and a sign that the Lord was 'pleased with our inheriting these parts . . . taking it from a people who had long usurped upon him, and abused his Creatures". Many of the Native Americans were forced into religion as the only other option was death.

Although not every protestant and Catholic missionary that came to the New World was participating in the same level of abuse, it was still prevalent among tribes. The vast majority of Christian missionaries did not recognize the customs of the Native peoples as spiritual or religious traditions in their right and many mission schools effectively removed Native young people from their cultures. Many Christian colonists and missionaries, even those most sympathetic to the lifeways of the Native peoples, categorized Native Americans as "heathen" who either accepted or resisted conversion to Christianity. They did not place Native American traditions under the protection of religious freedom that had been enshrined in the Constitution. It was not until 1978, almost 200 years after the Constitution was signed, that the American Indian Religious Freedom Act gave specific legal recognition to the integrity of Native American religions.

Where do we go from here?

Taking a look at the human tree in the soil of religion, we can see that there were clearly a lot of good fruits that were produced and continue to impact us into the modern era. The glories of the renaissance and Scientific Revolution are not to be taken lightly, as well as the founding of so many universities still in existence today. These good fruits completely changed the world and propelled the human tree out of the dark ages. Nonetheless, the human tree was not perfect and still produced bad fruits. Persecution against religious opponents was prevalent whether it be Native Americans in the New World or Muslims during the Crusades. Even Christians weren't free from the abusive systems of hierarchy and power imposed by the Roman Catholic Church through indulgences and relics. Seeing all of the bad fruit produced from the soil of religion, humanity was propelled into uprooting the tree completely and planting it in new soil. This new soil would do away with all of the religious ideas of the previous soil and would take the human mind and reason as ultimate authorities. The human tree would now spend some time in the soil of secularism.

3

THE SOIL OF SECULARISM

Born in the transition between eras, Rene Descartes would be the main commentator of the day in predicting the soil of secularism to come. Before Descartes's time, the Church was seen as the foundation of truth and they had a monopoly on it. Holding the Bible under lock and key, and the making of the infallible pope are just a few examples of their truth monopoly. Living through the time of the Protestant Reformation, Descartes observed the beginnings of a shift that was taking place. Reformers such as Martin Luther, John Calvin, and Ulrich Zwingli, had opened a can of worms and had begun to reshape the European mind towards religion. They showed that it was possible to go against the power of the Roman Catholic Church and that forced religion is a terrible thing.

By protesting the monopoly of truth that was the Church, they greatly opened Europeans up to the idea of freedom of thought, not being constrained by the powers of the day. Descartes saw this shift as an epistemological crisis, one that shook the very foundations of truth itself. Before this time, when asking the question "How do I know what is true?" the answer would be, "Whatever the Church says is true.". With the development of widespread freedom of thought, this was no longer the clear answer. This was one of the main reasons for the writing of one of Descartes's most famous works, *Meditations on First Philosophy* [1]. In the book, he felt that he must attempt to rebuild the house of truth on a sturdier foundation than the Church because it was losing authority.

In his first meditation, Descartes attempts to destroy the current house of knowledge using a methodology of doubt, something that was quite foreign to the thinking sphere in the age of religious soil. In this meditation, three increasingly strong skeptical arguments were put forward, calling everything into doubt. In meditation 2, after calling into doubt everything, he thinks of the one thing that he cannot doubt, which is the fact that he is thinking. Therefore, he sets the entire house of knowledge on the fundamental truth of "I think". His most famous phrase for which this work is known for is, "I Think therefore I am". From the foundation, he then rebuilt the entire house of knowledge on that sturdier foundation through deduction and logical arguments.

This marked a major shift in the methods of determining truth and waning of the authority and power of the Church. This ideological shift would soon be actualized in the soil to come, as the enlightenment and humanism movements would largely scrap the Church from the picture altogether. The human tree would now try out the soil of secularism, or non-religiosity.

The Good Fruit

The age of secularism was categorized by a transformation in the patterns of thought throughout the West, especially in places such as the would-be United States and other parts of western Europe. Many changes in political systems would be experimented with, wars would be fought, and much ink would be spilled over competing ideologies of how to run the world. Done with religion and the horrors that it had caused in the previous soil, the big thinkers of the soil of secularism would, for the most part, remove God from the equation and elevate man to take his place. Many good fruits came from this period of enlightened thought, which will be discussed in this section.

The Enlightenment

The most significant ideological revolution to take place during the secular soil was the Enlightenment. Spanning from 1685 to 1815, the Enlightenment spread quickly across Europe and the West as a time of radical reorientation of politics, science, philosophy, and communication. The thinkers behind this movement, John Locke, Thomas Hobbes, Charles Montesquieu, Jean-Jacques Rousseau, and many others, questioned authority and embraced the notion that humanity could be improved through rational change and reason alone. The Enlightenment produced numerous books, essays, inventions, scientific discoveries, laws, wars, and revolutions. While not a universally good fruit for everyone, the Enlightenment was largely an improvement to the previous patterns of thought and a great number of the ideas and books are highly influential today, many of which founded the very democratic government we experience in the United States as of now.

To fully understand the phenomenon that was the Enlightenment, an important distinction must be made. There were actually two strains of Enlightenment during this time, both with radically different ways of viewing the world. Enlightenment A as we will call it, built on the traditions of the religious soil and united it with the ancient Greek emphasis on reason and purpose. This Enlightenment held onto Judeo-Christian values that had bolstered throughout the West and claimed that reason was best united with a pursuit of morality and virtue. Among the thinkers that fall into this category are John Locke, Rene Descartes, and Gottfried Leibniz. Enlightenment B, also known as the radical Enlightenment by historians, attempted to separate reason and Judeo-Christian values and ethics. This strain of thought claimed that reason alone could govern the people and they rejected all religious authority. Proponents of this Enlightenment strain include Baruch Spinoza, David Hume, and Voltaire.

So which Enlightenment strain was better for society? Luckily, we don't have to guess, as history has played out both of these strains side by side and a clear winner has emerged. Both Enlightenment strains culminated in a revolution and a development of a new government system, but one would be filled with bloodshed and abuse of power, while the other would value the rights of the governed. By following closely in the reasoning and ethics of Enlightenment B, the French revolted against their monarchy and established a reign of terror that would cause immense bloodshed all in the name of reason. Following the unification of religion and reason that came with Enlightenment A, the United States drafted the Declaration of Independence and built a nation with inalienable rights for all people based on the fact that they were all made in God's image. The vast majority of the good fruit that came from the Enlightenment came from this strain of thinking.

In his essay titled *What is Enlightenment?* [2], Immanuel Kant addressed what would soon become the motto of the era "Dare to know! Have the courage to use your own reason!". The foundation of the Enlightenment was built upon the ideas of the scientific revolution, mainly those of Isaac Newton and John Locke. In Locke's famous *Essay Concerning Human Understanding*, he proposes that human nature was mutable, and that knowledge was gained from experience rather than some outside source. This was a radical change from the way that knowledge was gained before, as it was an appeal to experience and reason rather than the pope and the Church. Newton in his *Principia Mathematica* provided enlightenment thinkers with the calculus and math needed to give evidence for precisely measured change.

Immanuel Kant defined the Enlightenment as the "progress of mankind toward improvement" through the "freedom to make public use of one's reason on every point,". The age of reason, as it is sometimes called, built up the idea that critical thinking and reason is very important in all spheres of Western thought and culture. Doubt and new philosophy were being experimented with, and greater social changes were happening in the West.

Many of the greatest thinkers of this time such as Pierre Bayle advocated for the separation of Church and State, a philosophy that is still in effect in many countries today. This idea was spread through works such as John Locke's *Social Contract* [3], which stated that the government lacked authority in the realm of individual conscience and that they couldn't force religious belief. During the Enlightenment, many abolished the idea of heaven, instead of trying to make heaven on earth. This led to many cult and fringe groups emerging and gaining popularity as a means to bring this utopia to the people.

The greatest accomplishment of the Enlightenment was the political progress it produced. The success at explaining and understanding the natural world encouraged the Enlightenment project of re-making the social/political world, in accord with the models we allegedly find in our reason. This allowed for the age of the despot to come to a close, as is seen in the numerous revolutions of the time, which we will visit shortly. We owe to this period the basic model of government founded upon the consent of the governed; the articulation of the political ideals of freedom and equality and the theory of their institutional realization.

Much of our modern democratic thought owes its roots to the Enlightenment as do many of our current laws, judicial systems, and freedoms.

The Humanist Movement

With its roots in the Enlightenment, Humanism naturally flowed from the Enlightenment philosophies that elevated man and became the premier way of viewing humans at the time. Humanism is the stance and pattern of thought that emphasized the value and agency of mankind. This view elevated human progress and freedom, as well as held humans responsible for the promotion and development of individuals all over the world. This view naturally flowed from the increasing emphasis on human reason from the Enlightenment and the increased hope in human progress and development from the Scientific Revolution. The abolition of religion as a powerhouse also contributed to the rise of Humanism as now man had risen to take the very place that God once held in the West.

Not everything that came out of the Humanism movement was good, but it is undebatable that the increase in human rights, freedoms, and value during the movement was invaluable to our society today. While Humanism as an idea began in the high Renaissance period, with so many paintings and sculptures depicting the beauty of man, it continued into the enlightenment and expanded its scope. It was no longer just focused on visible representations of man as beautiful but took actions to increase the beauty in the lives of the actual man through increased freedoms, representation, and value.

One of the greatest things to come from a high view of humanity was the early documentation of universal human rights. Coming from the front lines of the French Revolution, The *Declaration of the Rights of Man and Citizen* was one of the earliest calls for universal human rights regardless of social status, something unheard of at the time. The Declaration of Independence is another example of this during the Humanist movement as it called for certain "unalienable rights for all man". This document was unique to any other document prior to it other than the Bible in claiming that all men are created equal and therefore have basic rights. In Rousseau's *Social Contract of 1762*, he argued that all government rested on a social contract (not on divine right, nor the Bible, nor tradition of any kind) in which "the assembled people" (democracy) determined everything. For him, "the person of the meanest citizen is as sacred and inviolable as that of the first magistrate" [3]; in other words, Rousseau insisted on complete equality (between men).

It is hard to argue that the Humanist movement was all bad for the West, as it gave birth to many of the greatest thinkers and value-enhancing ideas that the world had ever seen. The ideas of the Enlightenment of political reform and reason had become implemented into society through the Humanism movement. The death rate had decreased as they were riding on the back of many technological and scientific innovations of the Scientific Revolution.

The Bad Fruit

Slavery and the Limitation of Rights

While the Humanists did expand democratic rights greatly, these did not expand to all types of people, as women and blacks largely still had no vote or say in politics. With the increase in sea exploration, this period also saw the start of the Trans-Atlantic Slave Trade, the system of enslaving millions of Africans and selling them to plantation owners and others in the New World.

Many of the earliest calls for democracy such as the French *Declaration of The Rights of Man and Citizen* and the American Declaration of Independence only intended for democracy of white male landowners. It is because of this that Abigail Adams, the first lady to John Adams, wrote *Remember the Ladies*, a letter to Congress demanding an expansion of democratic rights to women. In France, when the question of religious minorities came up, the assembly readily agreed to grant full rights to Protestants but hesitated to do so for Jews. There were also property qualifications to vote in many of the early democracies.

The increase in wealth and democracy during this time was not self-sufficient. France and Great Britain were heavily dependent on their colonies for income. In the French colonies, free blacks had begun agitating for rights, but any such move was fiercely resisted by white planters, who feared it would undermine the entire slave system. This need for labor to keep all of the newly founded governments and revolutions going led to the rise of cheap slave labor.

Again, the human tree had produced bad fruit unknowingly. It would not be for at least another century later that slavery would be abolished in the United States and French colonies, and women would not receive representation for nearly two centuries. I'm sure I do not need to expound on the bad fruit of slavery as there are far better books and movies that depict the horrors that took place in the United States and elsewhere during the time of mass slavery. It is such a bad fruit that I could mention it in any of the soils of the human tree, as slavery is still prevalent today in many countries, and many countries in the Middle East and elsewhere still restrict rights for women. These issues aren't as directly related to the soil of secularism, however, so they will be left as brevities for the sake of conciseness.

The French Revolution

While many look upon history and see the French Revolution as a glorious event in which the peasants overturned the nobility and instated democracy, and while that is true, it would be a mistake to ignore the terrible bloodshed in the process. Sure, the French Revolution was a good thing for France, but it is also a microcosm of the phrase coined by Lord Acton: "Absolute power corrupts absolutely". The French Revolution saw the death of thousands of innocent civilians, all in the name of reason.

Beginning in 1789, the French Revolution was the culmination of radical Enlightenment thinking. It started as an innocent movement, in which the peasants or "third estate" as they were called in France, protested the shortage of bread in France. More problems for the French monarchy arose as the country was on the brink of bankruptcy because of the excessive spending of King Louis XVI. On top of this, the third estate, although comprising 98% of the population, could still be outvoted by the other two estates in the French pseudo-democratic "Estates General" system. It was a combination of these factors and more that led the third estate to revolt against the monarchy. The revolution escalated quickly as the third estate was able to mobilize and raid the Bastille for weapons. [4]

In November of 1793, after the execution of Louis XVI and his wife Marie-Antoinette by guillotine, a festival was held known as the Fête de la Raison or Festival of Reason. This festival came to represent all that the new republic of France would stand for and showed a radical shift from the soil of religion that was present in France not too long before. The festival began with transforming French churches into "Temples of Reason" and dismantling a Christian altar and replacing it with an altar to Liberty. A little girl was dressed up to be the so-called "Goddess of Reason" and was paraded around the streets as a symbol of the devotion of the French to their cause. Nobody could have predicted that the same streets on which the Goddess of Reason was paraded, would soon be covered in the blood of innocent French men and women.

The French Revolution soon took a turn for the worst and entered a period known by historians as the Reign of Terror. This was a period in which suspected enemies of the regime and political opponents were killed

by the thousands (not too dissimilar from our modern
"cancel culture" that destroys the careers of people who
don't buy into the mainstream political narrative). Although
the revolutionaries had abolished God, the actions of the
leaders in charge such as Maximillian Robespierre and the
Jacobin party were very god-like in application. As Gustave
Le Bon explains it in his book *The Psychology of
Revolution* [5],

"To the Jacobins of this epoch [the French Revolution], as
well as to those of our times, this popular entity constitutes
a superior personality possessing attributes peculiar to the
gods of never having to answer for their actions and never
making a mistake. Their wishes must be humbly acceded
to. The people may kill, burn, ravage, commit the most
frightening cruelties, glorify their hero today and throw him
into the gutter tomorrow, it is all the same; the politicians
will not cease to vaunt the people's virtues and to bow to
their every decision."

Their actions can be explained, at least in part by
their treatment of religion. They had abolished God and
even banned Christianity in the republic. After kicking God

off of his throne, they themselves took the throne of absolute power and truth, killing any that challenged it. They had embodied the very Enlightenment ideas and Humanism that were seen as great improvements of the time and made the ideas despicable.

The reign of terror, which only lasted about 10 months, killed over 27,000 French men, women, and children through public execution by guillotine. During the September Massacres, the French peasants launched an attack on the Catholic Church and killed 1,200 Christians in a matter of just 5 days. Commenting on the event, Jean François Ducis, a playwright at the time, stated: "Why talk to me of composing tragedies? Tragedy walks the streets. If I put my foot out of doors, I have blood up to my ankle".

Many other horrific events occurred during this time of championing reason as a god. One enemy of the revolution, Joseph Foulon de Doué, was executed, stuffed, and then paraded around the town on a stick. In Nantes, more than 1800 were executed via drowning in the river. The Princesse de Lamballe, a close friend of Marie

Antoinette, was literally ripped to pieces in the streets of
Paris.

So, how did the French Revolution, which started
out with lofty goals of liberty and independence, turn into a
bloodbath? One of the harshest critics of the French
Revolution at the time, Englishman Edmund Burke, had a
lot of ink to spill on the issue. Burke argued that the French
Revolution failed because it had ignored the lessons of
human nature, the morality of Christianity, and the
traditions of the past. Written at the onset of the revolution
in 1789, *Reflections on the Revolution in France* [6] became a
staple text in analysing the French revolution. In it he warns
of what the separation of past Christian values from reason
and government would do to the revolutionaries.

"The effect of liberty to individuals is that they may do
what they please; we ought to see what it will please them
to do, before we risk congratulations which may be soon
turned into complaints. Prudence would dictate this in the
case of separate, insulated, private men, but liberty, when
men act in bodies, is power".

The championing of reason and the death of God lead to one of the greatest takings of innocent blood that Europe had seen thus far in its history. The soil of secularism had spoiled with this event, as the abolition of religion was obviously not the clear answer to abolish the bad fruit of the human tree.

So, what's next?

It was obvious to many observers of the time that the human tree was still producing bad fruit in the soil of secularism. Abolishing religion, if anything, had increased the horrors of the bad fruits produced in its place. Because there was no God to rally behind, people were rallying behind tyrants such as Robespierre. Humanist ideas, however, would not fade away, but continue into the next soil of the human tree very prevalently. Instead of simply celebrating what humans were, the soil of technology would add another layer to the humanist movement. It was no longer simply a mindset of "look what man can become", but also "look what man can make". This would be a soil where continued innovation and technology would increase at a rate even faster than the Scientific Revolution. The human tree would soon be uprooted from the soil of secularism and planted firmly into the new soil of technology.

4

THE SOIL OF TECHNOLOGY AND INNOVATION

Although the secular experiment had failed the human race by giving birth to the horrors of the French Revolution and other dehumanizing events, it left a huge impact on the next human soil, that of technology and innovation. While still largely secular apart from a few great revival movements, the late 1800s and early 1900s witnessed the addition of another layer onto human society. Where in the Enlightenment, humans advanced intellectually, in the Industrial Revolution, humans advanced technologically. People were moving to cities by the thousands and fleeing from farm life in favor of life in the factories. Many young entrepreneurs made millions during this time by taking risks and investing and inventing new modes of energy, transportation, and healthcare. The Enlightenment ideas of human freedom couldn't have rung truer during this time, as many journeyed very far to vast frontiers in order to exercise their freedoms. The soil of Technology and Innovation was, for the most part, the most ambitious of the soils the human race had planted itself in, as the West was on the cutting edge of applying the ideas of the Enlightenment to progress human society with much trial and error. This effort was a large success as a lot of good fruit that can still be seen and impact us today was produced.

The Good Fruit

The Industrial Revolution

The first Industrial Revolution began in Great Britain in the late 1700s and early 1800s and therefore overlaps with the previous human soil. Since we are on the subject of a post-1800s world and the second industrial revolution occurred in the early 1900s, I will talk about both revolutions together as the second is largely a continuation of the first. Before the Industrial Revolution, the vast majority of people lived on farms and worked for a living wage either as the owner or a sharecropper. This began to change during the Industrial Revolution, where more and more factories were opening up and paying workers more money than a lifetime on the farm. This caused a great migration towards urban cities and places such as London, Boston, and New York City.

Production efficiency improved during the Industrial Revolution with inventions such as the steam engine. The steam engine dramatically reduced the time it took to manufacture products. More efficient production subsequently reduced prices for products—primarily due to lower labor costs—opening the marketing doors to a new level of customers. With more and more people being able to purchase and sell goods, the economy was starting to grow into the powerhouse we know of it today.

During the first Industrial Revolution, many new inventions and businesses were created that would be fundamental to the society of the time as well as our society today. It was during this time that electricity was discovered, and the lightbulb was invented by Thomas Edison. The first calculator was invented to help with mathematics, and the sewing machine made it easy to mass-produce clothing and other fabric goods. The X-ray and anesthesia were invented during this time to advance the state of medical affairs, and many general improvements to health standards such as care for water quality were implemented. The most influential of these inventions though was the steam engine. With its debut in 1786 by inventor James Watt, the steam engine made possible the industrial revolution by providing a way of compact energy to power the factories. This would also make it possible for the invention of automobiles and other forms of transportation in the second industrial revolution.

Beginning right after the end of the Enlightenment, the second Industrial Revolution started in 1870 and went through World War 1. The major inventions that made this second wave possible were interchangeable parts and a process of making steel known as the Bessemer Process. During this time, advancements in production and technology allowed for widespread adoption of technological innovations such as the telegraph, a telephone precursor, and railroad networks. This period saw the completion of the transcontinental railroad, which spanned the entirety of the United States and allowed people to travel further distances than ever before.

Improvements to healthcare spurred forwards during the Industrial Revolution and supported a larger population growth due to fewer deaths. Many medical instruments still in use today such as scalpels and modern microscopes saw mass production and dissemination, allowing for the increased effectiveness of doctors to heal patients. Many new cures to diseases also came out of this period such as the smallpox vaccine, and the pasteurization of water to disinfect it from Cholera. The entire London Sewage System was created during this time and the Metropolitan Water Act was passed to regulate the water supply. Death and infection rates from deadly diseases reached an all-time low during this period, as in the past these were unavoidable and caused the death of many citizens. Although many pollutants entered the air from factory smog, for the vast majority of people at the time, the industrial revolution greatly increased their quality of life.

Innovation in transportation such as the invention of the automobile in 1885 by Karl Benz (of whom the Mercedes Benz is named after) and Henry Ford, greatly helped to form our modern world, where cars are owned almost unanimously. In 1903, the Wright brothers invented the airplane and made possible quick intercontinental travel. This allowed for the greater sharing of ideas and the spread of innovations across country borders. The almost instantaneous messaging of the telegraph, invented by Alexander Gram Bell during this time, allowing people to send messages quickly across the country, a major necessity of our modernized world.

The economic and social impact of the Industrial Revolution is something that cannot be overstated. As a commentator of the day put it, "The economic changes that have occurred during the last quarter of a century -or during the present generation of living men- have unquestionably been more important and more varied than during any period of the world's history". Crop failures no longer produced mass starvation and death during this period because of the vast industrial framework that society had taken on. The factory system centralized production in separate buildings funded and directed by specialists. The division of labor made both unskilled and skilled labor more productive and led to the rapid growth of the population in industrial centers. The shift away from agriculture toward industry had occurred in Britain by the 1730s, when the percentage of the working population engaged in agriculture fell below 50%, a development that would only happen elsewhere in the 1830s and '40s. By 1890, the figure had fallen to under 10% and the vast majority of the British population was urbanized.

The good fruit of innovation, technology, and increased lifespan and quality of life for millions of people wouldn't last too long. The Industrial Revolution, in addition to directly producing its own inequalities and abuses of workers in factories, would make possible largescale wars such as World Wars 1 and 2. It would allow for more destruction than anyone could have thought possible by the human hand. The phrase "look what man can do" had taken a wholly different approach by the end of the soil of technology and innovation, as the good fruit had by then spoiled.

The Bad Fruits

Factory Abuses

Though a lot of good fruit came from the factories, many of these "model workplaces" were actually very abusive to their workers. As factories and businesses were being built up from the ground, they needed a lot of workers to assist them. Many of these workers were desperate for work and were willing to labor for any amount of money. Factories took advantage of this and paid workers very little. People worked fourteen to sixteen hours a day for six days a week, but the majority were unskilled workers, who only received about $8-$10 dollars a week, working at approximately 10 cents an hour. Even skilled workers only received a little bit more than unskilled workers. Women received one-third or sometimes one-half of the pay that men received. Children received even less.

Owners, who were only concerned with making a profit, were satisfied because labor costed less.

Usually, factories also had very little light and the only light that would come in would be the sunlight through the windows. Many factories used the newly fashioned steam engines and machines that spit out smoke when used, and many workers came home covered in soot by the end of the day. The machines they used were largely not up to safety code and workers took very little safety precautions as there were no standards at the time. This led to many accidents occurring with the machines as some would mutilate limbs, or even kill workers when malfunctioning. One of the workers in the British parliament at the time commented:

"There are factories, no means few in number, nor confined to the smaller mills, in which serious accidents are continually occurring, and in which, notwithstanding, dangerous parts of the machinery are allowed to remain unfenced." [1]

Children were paid less than 10 cents per hour and many developed physical malformities because of the hard labor and lack of sunlight and rest. Many times, children were preferred to adult workers because they could fit into small cervices and spaces that adults could not. Child labor was abundant and estimates even show that over 50% of the British workforce in 1870 was under 14 years old. Over 750,000 children under 14 in America were working as of 1870 as well. The horrors that children in the factories experienced was captured well in a memoir to a certain Mary Richards, who died in a factory at the age of 10.

"A girl named Mary Richards, who was thought remarkably pretty when she left the workhouse, and, who was not quite ten years of age, attended a drawing frame, below which, and about a foot from the floor, was a horizontal shaft, by which the frames above were turned. It happened one evening when her apron was caught by the shaft. In an instant, the poor girl was drawn by an irresistible force and dashed on the floor. She uttered the most heart-rending shrieks! The factory overseer ran towards her, an agonized and helpless beholder of a scene of horror. He saw her whirled round and round with the shaft - he heard the bones of her arms, legs, thighs, etc. successively snap asunder, crushed, seemingly, to atoms, as the machinery whirled her round, and drew tighter and tighter her body within the works, her blood was scattered over the frame and streamed upon the floor, her head appeared dashed to pieces - at last, her mangled body was jammed in so fast, between the shafts and the floor, that the water being low and the wheels off the gear, it stopped the main shaft. When she was extricated, every bone was found broken - her head dreadfully crushed. She was carried off quite lifeless."[2]

When many of the workers died at the hands of the machines, they received the blame for their death. There was very little accountability and rarely did anyone publicly question whether the working conditions and lack of safety standards had anything to do with the high number of on-the-job accidents. Even the newspapers of the time found a way to blame the victim and in one account, after a screw factory worker was killed by a machine, the Boston Herald said that the death was due to his "over assurance of his ability". Other newspapers also condemned him for his carelessness and lack of knowledge operating the machine.

Most factories also had a problem with exploding boilers which killed about 50,000 people every year.

Many died in order to industrialize the West, but nobody would've predicted what that industrialization would have come to. In pursuit of increasing technology, the workers would create advanced weapons, bullets, tanks, and many other weapons of mass destruction. With advances in chemistry, mustard gas and nuclear bombs were created. A period of great progress also brought one of the most backsliding and progress defeating events in all of history: the two World Wars.

World Wars 1 And 2

With the onset of technology, it was inevitable that wars would become much more deadly and destructive. Before this time period, wars were fought almost exclusively with infantry, cavalry, and the occasional cannon. Firearms were weak and nearly all of them were single shot and took a while to reload. There was no chemical warfare, tanks, planes, missiles, or weapons of mass destruction. The Industrial Revolution changed this premise. The same technology that gave us the automobile gave us the tank. The same technology that gave the Wright brothers flight also gave us the means to drop bombs and missiles on innocent cities. The same technology that gave us advances in medicine to save many lives, gave us the means to end many lives as well with the onset of mustard gas. World war 1 and 2 would be the ultimate bad fruit of the soil of technology whose impact is still felt very much today.

In World War 2 alone, an estimated 70-85 million people perished (about 3% of the world population at the time), and in World War 1, 20 million died including 9.7 million civilians. At the end of both World Wars, 70% of European industrial buildings had been destroyed and the economy was in ruins. In the Soviet Union alone, over 1,700 cities lay in ruin. Germany was divided into two countries, separating families and loved ones, and the war took an overall toll on every citizen.

To demonstrate the vast destruction caused by technology at the time, we can look no further than the effects of the war on two particular cities. Before the war, Hiroshima and Nagasaki were important military cities with a bustling economy and a dense concentration of people in the city centers. The population of Hiroshima had reached a peak of over 380,000 earlier in the war but before the atomic bombing, the population had steadily decreased because of a systematic evacuation ordered by the Japanese government. At the time of the attack, the population was approximately 255,000. Nagasaki was similar in size as well. After the bombing of these two cities however, all of the man-made progress came tumbling down as they were reduced to rubble. The time it took to transform from a great city into a ruinous wasteland was less than 10 minutes. As one of the pilots of the US planes recounts it,

"The bomb burst with a blinding flash and a huge column of black smoke swirled up toward us. Out of this column of smoke there boiled a great swirling mushroom of gray smoke, luminous with red, flashing flame, that reached to 40,000 feet in less than 8 minutes. Below through the clouds, we could see the pall of black smoke ringed with fire that covered what had been the industrial area of Nagasaki" [3]

Even more horrific were the concentration camps, meant for Jews, gypsies, and other political enemies of the Third Reich. Over 6 million Jews alone died in the camps, many of either the gas chambers or starvation. I will not even attempt to recount the terrible things that happened inside the camps, but one only needs to read Anne Frank's diaries or Eli Wiesel's *Night* to grasp the abomination.

The wars had turned morality in Europe on its head and the line between right and wrong became blurred. Hitler was even using religious figures such as Martin Luther to back up his claims of racial superiority. One German novelist at the time Erich Maria Remarque says it best.

"A crude age. Peace is stabilized with cannon and bombers, humanity with concentration camps and pogroms. We're living in a time when all standards are turned upside-down, Kern. Today the aggressor is the shepherd of peace, and the beaten and hunted are the troublemakers of the world. What's more, there are whole races who believe it!" [4]

All conception of human progress that developed during the soil of technology was shattered in the World Wars. The greatest inventions of the time had also turned out to be the greatest devices of destruction. The greatest advances in technology such as atomic physics and chemistry caused the complete annihilation of two Japanese cities. The great factories that used to make clothes and automobiles now had turned into bombs and bullet churning machines. The phrase "look what man can do" had become quite ironic, as mankind had just undone much of the progress it had made. This would constitute a radical uprooting and shift in the soil after the war. For many, hopelessness prevailed, as they were done with the horrors of the war and went to search for meaning elsewhere. This next soil would nearly become the opposite of the previous, as people would leave the factory in favor of the commune and leave technology in favor of drugs. The human tree would once again be uprooted from the soil of technology and innovation and placed promptly into the soil of love and peace.

5

THE SOIL OF LOVE AND PEACE

After experiencing the bad fruits of the horrific
World Wars, many left the factories to go live on hippie
communes. While not as widespread as many of these other
soils, the hippie movement was still large enough to boast a
significant following and enact change in the government.
The large majority of Americans weren't openly hippies
and didn't live on the communes, but they sympathized
with the goals and motivations of the movement, especially
protesting wars. A few decades after the World Wars, the
United States would embark on the very unpopular
Vietnam war, in which the hippies played a dominant role
in fighting against.

As people, the hippies of the 60s were strange. With the newly popular rock music, many developed their own culture, clothing, and routines. Many grew their hair out very long, wearing bright colored clothing with baggy pants, and many were avid consumers of rock, funk, and psychedelic music. The key characteristic shared by all hippies was the drive to be authentic. All of the culture around them, they believed, was just following corrupt systems and conforming to the world. They wanted to do their own thing and live their own life, which is why many traveled from the main city to live in the countryside with others like them. A description of the hippie, as written in a TIME magazine article titled "The Hippies: A philosophical subculture" [1] was understood as "Do your own thing, wherever you have to do it and whenever you want. Drop out. Leave society as you have known it. Leave it utterly. Blow the mind of every straight person you can reach. Turn them on, if not to drugs, then to beauty, love, honesty, fun.".

Another factor leading to the rise of the hippie was the extremely comfortable and conformist culture of the 1950s. While it could be said to be a soil of its own, the consumerism of the 50s became a key component in every soil thereafter. Consumerism is just as lively if not more so today than in the 50s, but in the 50s it was the main goal and focus of the middle-class American. The opening of suburbs and the early beginnings of television and radio helped people escape from the previous horrors of war. The counterculture was really in essence countering this form of culture because they were largely against consumerism and many hippies sold most of their belongings and donated all their money before going to live on the hippie communes. The contrast between these cultures could not have been greater, as hippies lived with very little in the form of material pleasures and focused more on the spiritual or soul. The hippies didn't buy houses in suburbia, but rather, settled for living in RVs and vans out in the desert. It was truly a unique way of living that produced many good and bad fruits.

The Good Fruit

Peace, Love, and Community

Most humans alive can agree that these three things, peace, love, and community, are by themselves very good and honorable qualities of a society. Many Americans at the time had just come from the warzone, a place where there was no peace, so it was a very sought-after characteristic of the time. The infamous "peace sign" was developed during the hippie era to symbolize this key characteristic of hippie culture and it was present on vans, shirts, and signs throughout America.

The famous slogan "Make love not war" was popularized during this time as well, and the hippies by and large practiced what they preached. The anti-war sentiments weren't just held by the hippies alone, but extended to many college campuses and even Americans living in suburbia. After America's involvement in Vietnam, which began in 1955, millions of hippies and Americans took to the streets to protest. Many famous anti-war songs came out of this period of protest such as "What Are You Fighting For?" by Phil Ochs, Marvin Gaye's "What's Going On?", and Joan Baez's "Saigon Bride". The anti-war movement gained immense popularity not only from college campuses and hippies, but from many prominent artists, authors, and preachers, with Martin Luther King Jr. also supporting it. In his antiwar sermon "Beyond Vietnam", King Jr. stated,

"We have destroyed their two most cherished institutions: the family and the village. We have destroyed their land and their crops. We have cooperated in the crushing of the nation's only non-communist political force, the unified Buddhist Church. We have supported the enemies of the peasants of Saigon. We have corrupted their women and children and killed their men." [2]

These protests of peace and love eventually ended the war in Vietnam, as by the 1970s the popularity of the war had declined significantly, and the Americans were fighting without much success. The hippie values of peace and love had prevailed, and many celebrated this victory. With nothing left to protest however, the hippie movement lost favor and numbers, becoming a fringe community thereafter.

Another good fruit of the hippie movement was the deep sense of community that many felt while being a part of life on the communes. Everyone shared everything and there were general stores that gave families what they needed. Men would often work in fields, while women would work in the community meeting needs and caring for the children. Many friends became like family and the commune's purpose was to make everyone a giant family. While many felt the good fruit of community, others didn't and would end up either leaving or attempting to leave the communes.

To some, the commune was a utopia, to others, quite the opposite. Many observers today equate the communes with a cult-like lifestyle, one that basically enforced communism and kept all of the members in poverty. This is partially true, as many communes did function like a cult, but in many ways, they were quite different. At the center of the community was a group of people who just wanted to escape from the consumer society and live free from rules and regulations. While this good fruit lasted for a little while, it became corrupted and led to our modern lens by which we now view hippies. A group that was originally formed to protest the war and society soon gave in to the very pleasures that they were protesting, drugs and violence soon followed.

The Bad Fruit

Drugs and Open Love

When many think of hippies today, drugs are on their minds, especially psychedelics such as LSD. This is not an incorrect way of thinking as many hippies did indulge in copious amounts of drugs during their lifetime as part of their method to escape from society. Many justified their use as a way to expand consciousness. A popular book during this time *The Psychedelic Experience* reported the therapeutic benefits of LSD and other psychedelics with the main idea being that you can take psychedelics to enter a different state of consciousness and thus heal the wounds of the past. This was attractive to many young teens living on the communes and drugs became immensely popular. As Jay Stevens, a historian of the time put it in his book, *Storming Heaven: LSD and the American Dream* [3]:

"According to the hippies, LSD was the glue that held the Haight together. It was the hippie sacrament, a mind detergent capable of washing away years of social programming, a re-imprinting device, a consciousness-expander, a tool that would push us up the evolutionary ladder."

Many in the 70s thought of drugs as glamorous, without side effects and harm to the body. The book *The Truth About Drugs -- The Body, Mind, And You* [4] by Gene Chill and John Duff asserted that drugs such as cocaine weren't addictive and were beneficial to take. Once the drugs started taking over the hippie communes, many lost their initial vision of community and purpose in life thus reverting to physical pleasure, just like the culture around them. As one observer recognized "there seemed nothing "counter" about this culture".

Drug abuse in the hippie culture led to many other physical cases of abuse in the search for pleasure. One popular hippie slogan that appeared during this time was "If it feels good, do it!". This was the thinking that was behind the massive drug use and also a lot of the policies of "open love" that happened in the communes. This thinking encouraged spontaneous sexual activity and experimentation among members of the commune. The idea of strictly monogamous relationships, especially sexual ones, went out of the window. The open relationship became a hallmark of the hippie lifestyle and this went largely hand and hand with psychedelic experimentation. As one observer put it "Free love made the whole love, marriage, sex, baby package obsolete". Love was no longer limited to one person and was free to give to everyone. This idea, which is seemingly good on paper, led to the abuse of many women in the communes and corruption of the common view of marriage.

While the vast majority of hippies were completely against violence, there was no shortage of violent episodes in the community. During the "Summer of Love", a meetup in 1967 of many prominent counterculture musicians and hippies, many of the young hippies violently took to the streets after the event. Many were without a place to live so they lived on the streets where malnourishment, drug addiction, and disease. Crime and violence in the streets skyrocketed as these people were without hope and disillusioned by psychedelics.

The good fruits produced by the human tree had again become spoiled in the soil of love and peace, two things that are in themselves good qualities. As in the soil of religion, the soil of love and peace saw the perversion of even the most virtuous of human characteristics. What started as a group of people protesting the war, had warped into a movement of drug use, violence, and open love that negated the very purpose of the movement altogether. The countercultural hippies had become the very pleasure-seeking people they had tried to counter. Their pursuit of drugs was no different than everyone else at the time seeking after consumer goods and fancy cars. The soil that the human tree was planted in would once again, disappoint, as bad fruits were produced.

At this point in the story of human history, it seems as though nothing was quite working out. This, however, would not stop humanity from trying, as after uprooting itself from the soil of love and peace, it planted itself in the soil of economics. This would be a period of large economic growth, especially for the United States, as capitalism took the throne and was treated as a godlike figure in comparison to the opposing communism of the Soviet Union. Would this soil be good enough to sustain the human tree? We will soon see as we explore the soil of economics.

6

THE SOIL OF ECONOMICS

A criticism might be made at this point in the book that many of these so-called "soils" happened at the same time and are present throughout history. This is a valid statement and true in most senses. Religion didn't magically die out in the age of secularism, as many enlightenment thinkers were religious. Secularism didn't completely disappear with the onset of technology, and neither did technology disappear after the wars. In fact, it continues to advance to this day. This book only purports to be a metaphor, giving generalities and not specifics. While these soils are continuous, they aren't always the main components at a given time. For instance, in the age of secularism, while religion was still there, it was of much less of a focus and importance as in the age of religion. This can be compared to actual soil at this point. Soil is not a homogenous thing and consists of many different particles and nutrients. Some soils may contain a certain percentage of silt or sand, while others contain mostly clay. One soil could have 48% nitrogen content, while another has only 7%. This is precisely how we are classifying the "soils" in this book. The majority of the soil component classifies the entirety of the soil for ease of the metaphor. I do know that this method is not the most realistic and does not conform to the complexities of real life, but the main goal of this book isn't to give the most accurate and precise history of the human race. There are thousands of other books out there written by famous historians that could give you that. We are here to do something very different, something that transcends mere facts and timelines.

I explain all of this to justify the placing of the "soil of economics" after the soil of love and peace. These soils for the most part coexisted in human history, but the soil of economics slightly outlived the hippie movement and pushed into the early 2000s. This period saw the clashing of two worldwide economic systems, warring against each other for followers. It saw a focus on big business and the stock market like never before in human history, and the role of government in society came as one of the biggest questions of the day. It was these characteristics and more that classified the 1980s to 2000 as the soil of economics.

After World War 2, most of the West was in ruins. The war had been fought all across Europe, so many cities were completely destroyed or ransacked. From the many bombings of civilian populations, thousands of industrial buildings were reduced to rubble and the economies of these cities were destroyed. A long period of rebuilding would need to start in Europe, especially for the now divided Germany which took the biggest hit from losing the war. The only two major countries that didn't receive such an economic burden were the Soviet Union and the United States, who both emerged as superpowers after the war. This was largely because the war had, for the most part, not been fought on their own turf and their own cities weren't bombed too badly, with the exception of certain Soviet cities and of course Pearl Harbor. These two powers would shape the world-to-come in the soil of economics.

The two battling economic systems at the time were the Capitalism of the West and the Communism of the

East. Each system was power-hungry, and many military campaigns would occur to expand the ideas of economics further around the globe. Before we go further, it may be helpful to quickly explain the differences in economics that made these two systems so different from each other, so much so that many were willing to go to war to not have the other prevail.

Capitalism, an idea coined by Adam Smith's *Wealth of Nations* [1], was the idea that the private sphere should control the economy, with every individual business controlling profits, prices, and competition. The Capitalist system of running the economy was by no means just invented during this soil, as it built on enlightenment ideals and roots of individual liberty and freedom. This was a hands-off method of doing economics and the government played a small role in maintaining the economy. The Capitalist form of economics was termed laissez-faire (French for "allow to do") meaning a form of economics without intervention from the government.

Communism, on the other hand, was quite the opposite. It was the idea that the public sphere should control the economy, with the government controlling profits, prices, competition, and distribution of wealth. It was a system intended to help the impoverished people of the Soviet Union by distributing wealth equally among all citizens and stealing from the rich. This idea was popularized by Karl Marx in his *Communist Manifesto* [2], where he laid out the principals of class struggle and public land ownership. Unlike Capitalism, Communism had a large role for the government to play and therefore, most communist countries at the time had dictatorships to fill these roles.

As you can see, these systems were polar opposite ways to run a society and an economy. It was these differences that would largely contribute to the start of the Cold War, a period of animosity between the Soviet Union and the United States of America. Many wars such as the Vietnam War would be fought in the name of Capitalism and many lives were lost for this simple idea and its expansion. War was not the only thing that marked this period, as the push for economic growth and focus, at least in the United States, would also produce a lot of good fruits

that contribute greatly to how we manage our economy
today.

The Good Fruit

Prosperity of the Peoples

The period after World War 2 saw one of the
greatest boosts in Gross Domestic Product (GDP) that the
United States had ever experienced. From the end of the
war to the early 70s, the GDP of the United States had
increased from $228 billion to $1.7 trillion. This period saw
a great increase in the middle class of America, as
employment rates were high, there was a housing boom
with more affordable housing in the suburbs, and many
corporations profited greatly during this time.

A large improvement to infrastructure was a focal
point of internal economic improvements of this time. In
the late 50s, Eisenhower authorized the Interstate Highway
System, which built highways through most of the states

and greatly improved the ability to travel on an interstate level. Over 64,000 km of highways were built during this time. This led many more Americans to travel to the Southwest, causing suburbs outside of major Southwestern cities such as Phoenix and Los Angeles to begin to form and become populated.

Another factor contributing to increased prosperity was the military-industrial complex created by the tensions of the Cold War. Many factories filled with workers were needed to produce tanks, planes, and warships to threaten the Soviet Union if they were to ever attack. This led to an increase in jobs in an industry that is not so readily active today or during a time of peace.

A so-called "New Class" of Americans had arisen during this time as described in John Kenneth Galbraith's *Affluent Society* [3], a popular book in the early 60s. He argued that this new class was "highly educated business and professional people for whom work was no longer dirty and menial, but interesting and rewarding". Many members of this new class now saw things such as plumbing, entertainment, and personal transportation as staple things that everyone should have. A few decades ago, these would have been foreign concepts, but in the soil of economics, all was possible.

Social welfare also expanded during this period, especially under Lyndon B. Johnson's plan for a "Great Society". Programs such as Social Security started at this time, as well as retirement and unemployment pensions. Supplemental Security Income was also instated by Nixon and this helped to aid the blind, deaf, and people with other disabilities. During his presidency, he also increased the ability of the poor to get food stamps. Other legislation passed during the Nixon Administration included the Rehabilitation Act (1973), the Education for All Handicapped Act (1975), the Health Maintenance Act (1973), the Family Planning Services and Population Act (1974), the Occupational Safety and Health Act (1970), the Juvenile Justice and Delinquency Act (1974), and the Child Abuse Prevention Act (1974). All of these helped to greatly improve the social wellbeing of American citizens as well as ensure prosperity for the large majority at the time.

All of these factors led to an America, and pretty soon after, a Europe that was prosperous and well-developed. Of course, this was a much different story on the East, as conditions in the Soviet Union did not improve immediately after the war under the Communist system. Many would still live in poverty, consumer goods were few and far between, and political enemies were sentenced to life in the Gulags, or work camps to die. You must remember, however, that this book is largely focused on the West, so we must not let the bad fruit of the East contaminate that of the West. Prosperity in the West was great, but it didn't come without its consequences. The banner of Capitalism soon turned into corruption and the chase for wealth left behind many in abject poverty [4].

The Bad Fruit

Corruption and Expansion

A defining event of the bad fruit of the soil of economics was the infamous Watergate Scandal. While countless other scandals took place during this time period, and probably many that to this day we do not know about, Watergate tends to attract the attention of all because it was a scandal of the presidency, the leading head of the United States. It not only hurt those involved but shattered the high view of government and the economic state of many Americans. If you do not know exactly what this scandal was or need some help remembering, there are countless good movies, books, and even a board game titled "Watergate" if you need a refresher. But the short one in this book might suffice for you.

The Watergate scandal began early on the morning of June 17, 1972, when several burglars were arrested in the office of the Democratic National Committee, located in the Watergate complex of buildings in Washington, D.C. This was no ordinary robbery: The prowlers were connected to President Richard Nixon's re-election campaign, and they had been caught wiretapping phones and stealing documents. In August, Nixon gave a speech in which he swore that his White House staff was not involved in the break-in. Most voters believed him, and in November 1972 the president was re-elected in a landslide victory. At this time, two investigators from the Washington Post looked into the case further and found Nixon and many of his collaborators guilty of an abuse of power. Many of the co-conspirators were thrown into federal prison and Nixon resigned, knowing he would soon be impeached.

This abuse of power was just one of the major corruptions that came with such a heavy focus on wealth and power during this time. Many large companies such as Kellogg's, BAE Systems, and Siemens AG were involved in taking governmental bribes and paying off government officials in order to bypass the law or get laws to rule in their favor. Many of the government officials complied because of the large sums of money many of these corporations were able to pay them, sometimes upward of $100 million. The chase for wealth had left many to compromise morals to get to the top of the food chain.

This also meant that there was a large inequality in wealth during this period as well. Income inequality during the 70s and 80s was higher than it had ever been in American history. The stock market was indeed booming, but the amount of share held by the bottom 90% of the wealthiest citizens was only 23%. It was a period of "the rich get richer" and while there was an immense improvement in the lives of many middle-class citizens as well, the movement away from cities and into suburbs left the cities to be homes to rundown living complexes and an increasing amount of homelessness.

Along with economic corruption during this time, comes the beast of foreign oppression that was caused in the name of Capitalism and democracy. The Cold War had provoked many countries to be forced to pick a side, especially if they had a trade interest or political relationship with either superpower nation. Many revolutions for independence took place during this period, and there was a constant fear in the eyes of American leaders that these revolutions would lead to Communist governments in allegiance to the Soviet Union. After World War 2, many Latin American countries were starting to develop and change their governmental systems. Many interventions were made by the United States in these countries to protect its economic interests and to stabilize the workers because if the workers aren't revolting, then the US business interests aren't in danger.

The United States, in protecting business interests and their Capitalist dreams, promoted the protection and support of many corrupt governments in Latin America specifically. In Argentina, the democratically elected president Isabel Perón was overthrown by a US-supported coup d'état, and Perón was replaced by military dictator Jorge Videla. During his period as a leader, many human rights were violated as extrajudicial arrests, mass executions, torture, rape, disappearances of political prisoners and dissenters, and illegal relocations of children. A similar coup d'état was supported in Brazil in order to overthrow a socialist-leaning president that had been elected by the people. In Chile, after the democratic election of President Salvador Allende, the CIA got involved in supporting another coup d'état against the government because of Allende's supposed socialist leanings. What followed was the decade's long reign of the US-supported dictatorship of Augusto Pinochet. In El Salvador, to protect American economic interests such as the United Fruit Company, rebellions were crushed that were trying to overthrow anti-democratic governments and oligarchies. In Paraguay, the US implemented dictator

Alfredo Stroessner, whose rule lasted 35 years and made Paraguay one of the poorest countries in Latin America.

Many more of these stories could be given, as the United States was involved in nearly every Latin American country during the Cold War. The desire for wealth and power had expanded even beyond the American border and the corruption that went with that desire expanded with it. The number of terrible things instated by these dictatorships caused many of these Latin American countries to be impoverished and far behind the rest of the West in development.

We are for the most part still in this struggle and trying to deal with the bad fruit that came from the soil of economics. Many third world and Latin American countries, those who didn't take a side in the Cold War, are still impoverished today. Corruption still exists within the government and big organizations. There has been a shift however, in the cultural image and thought towards these big businesses and corporations. More and more people, especially college students, have become dissatisfied with the American dream of getting rich quickly at the expense of all others. Many efforts and protests have gone into lowering the wage gap and diminishing the oppression that the rich supposedly have on society. Many of the wealthiest citizens are now under fire for sexual assault and the very fact that you are wealthy diminishes your appeal to the general public. The soil that once held the big business model and an elevated view of the economy is starting to diminish. It is being and has been largely replaced by a soil that cares about the equal outcomes of all people and ideas, even if those ideas aren't the greatest. The banner of wealth that was once waved in the soil of economics has been replaced with the banner of tolerance and equality. The opposition has changed from being countries that were sympathetic to Communism, to those who claim to have exclusive truth and don't support full inclusion. The human tree would undergo another replanting from the soil of economics to the soil of postmodernism.

7

THE SOIL OF POSTMODERNISM

If you've heard the phrases "follow your heart", "just be authentic", "that's true for you, but not for me", "don't judge", and "there is no wrong answer" in the popular media, then you've probably lived through the soil of postmodernism. This soil, which is starting to slowly fade away, was very prevalent from the early 2000s to about the time that Trump got elected in 2016. This is the dominant message promoted throughout many Disney movies, popular YouTube channels such as Buzzfeed and Vox, and even many spiritual/religious movements. In order to fully understand where the postmodernist soil came from, we must first understand modernism.

Modernism was popularized by Descartes who was called "the father of modernism". It is a way of doing philosophy and self-evaluation that is best explained with a map metaphor. If you imagine your entire life as a map, then doing philosophy is map revision. This metaphorical map is possessed by everyone and helps us to navigate the world. It tells us what we can and can't know, what's real in the world, where we are in this world, and what role we play. This map for the most part is formed by our upbringing, as it is rare that you can simply craft your own map of the world from scratch. Philosophy's main goal in this analogy is to examine your current map and make improvements, or revisions that more correctly align with the truth. We do this based on the ancient wisdom put forth by Socrates when he said, "the unexamined life is not worth living". To what extent you can revise your map, however, is the main divide between modernism and postmodernism. To a modernist like Descartes, you can completely transcend the map and select a new one, scrapping even the foundations of the old map. This is largely what he did in his *Meditations on First Philosophy*, as he deconstructed the map that had the Church as the foundation of knowledge and then selected a new map with the foundation of "I think". Postmodernism differs in that it states that you can only make map revisions from inside the map itself. You must stay on the map to revise it and cannot transcend the map. It denies the idea of absolute truth and metanarratives (the grand overarching story of life). Since you cannot transcend the map, postmodernists say, all truth becomes relative to other points on the map rather than being absolute such as in a modernist approach. [1]

This brings us to the soil of postmodernism in our modern era. Coming from the time of empiricism and technological advance of the 20th century, the postmodern soil represents a radical shift. To understand how this shift took place, there is an overarching trend in history that can begin to make sense of the soil of relativism, and even the soil that will come after it (but we won't spoil that now). This historical trend functions like a cycle and has been going on for centuries now, as humanity searches for meaning and purpose in the universe. The cycle begins with a corrupted form of religion. This can be any form of Christianity or other religion that drives people away from the truth and leaves them with a sour taste in their mouths. For a great example of this, just look back to the bad fruits of chapter 2. After people have such a sour taste of religion in their mouth, they will turn to a phase of "optimistic reductivism". This is the sentiment that states "God is dead and now the creature is to be praised". This was what was going on during the enlightenment as the humanist movement was making it into the mainstream and mankind was in the spotlight. After a while of this optimism however, people begin to figure out that moral values and the false sense of purpose that they have created is absurd. This marks the phase shift into "pessimistic reductivism", where God is still dead, but now values have been blurred and life has no meaning and is quite absurd. This sentiment became popular in the 1900s with the nihilist movement that accompanied the World Wars. These wars made people greatly lose their hope in the goodness of mankind and human achievement. Many proponents of this view were among the most educated of their time, such as Joseph Conrad, and Albert Camus. In the words of Camus himself,

"When it comes to man's most basic questions of meaning and purpose, the universe is silent. When I wrote the Myth of Sisyphus, I tried to show that all human attempts to answer the questions of meaning are futile… In a word, our very existence is absurd… So, what do you do? For me, the only response was… to commit suicide, intellectual suicide, or physical suicide… To lose one's life is only a little thing. But, to lose the meaning of life, to see our reasoning disappear, is unbearable. It's impossible to live a life without meaning". [2]

The nihilist movement largely eliminated meaning from life and left its followers in utter hopelessness. These sentiments cannot exist in a flourishing humanity, however, because one of the most basic needs of humankind is a will to meaning, as described by Viktor Frankl, award-winning psychiatrist during WW2. After surviving four concentration camps, Frankl observed that the "will to meaning" was the number one factor that contributed to the chance of survival for the prisoners. Those who did not have a reason for living simply couldn't survive the suffering of the camps. He emerged from the camps as a firm believer in the phrase coined by Fredrich Nietzsche a few decades earlier: "He who has a 'why' to live can bear almost any 'how'".

Since humankind desperately needs meaning, and they couldn't find it in the objective world around them, the subjective movement was born, which would eventually become the postmodernism we know today. Since objectivity was meaningless to them, subjectivity was the only way to find meaning and purpose in life. Many in this period as you will soon see, made up their own meaning for life and to go against that meaning was deemed intolerant, rude, or just plain unacceptable. The sentiments of this final phase can be summed up in the words of Dave Williams, the lead singer of a band known as Drowning Pool. "Everybody needs something, you know. If it's Jesus, if its Satan, if its alcohol, if its music, whatever." [3]

It is this historical cycle that brought about the postmodern soil and can help us to understand the deep roots of how it all began. The hopelessness and lack of meaning in life after the great wars left humanity to search for its own meaning in this world.

How Do You Find Truth in This Soil?

Epistemology is a big word to describe the simple question of "How do you know what is true?". Many different answers have been given to this question throughout history, and each soil tends to have its unique way of finding truth. In the soil of religion, the answer was "whatever the church says is true". In the secular soil, it was "whatever we can come up with using our reason". In the soil of technology, it was "whatever the scientists and world leaders tell us". In the soil of love and peace, it was "whatever spreads the core values of love and peace and goes against cultural conformism". In the soil of economics, it was "whatever the government says". In the soil of postmodernism, the main way of determining what is true is "my feelings say so".

This way of finding truth has been widespread in popular media, particularly in the most recent Disney movies. There is no shade being thrown at these movies, as I think they portray plenty of good values and are quite entertaining, but this one particular value is one that I have seen propagated in recent years of development. One of Walt Disney's most famous quotes that spread this epistemology of "follow your heart", and what has been one of the main inspirations behind places like Disneyland is this: "If you can dream it, you can do it". Quotes from movies such as "Let your heart guide you; it whispers so listen closely" from Land Before Time, and "No matter how your heart is grieving, if you can keep believing, the dream that you wish will come true" from Cinderella, give the viewer an airy sense that their heart is the source of all truth. In Cinderella 2, one of the songs is even explicitly titled "Follow Your Heart".

In the "follow your heart" epistemology, truth becomes relative, as everyone has different hearts as a basic biological fact. The phrase "it is true for you, but not true for me" is commonly heard when talking about the soil of postmodernism. The sentiments are best expressed in the words of Gandhi when he said "Nobody in this world possesses absolute truth. Relative truth is all we know. Therefore, we can only follow the truth as we see it. Such pursuit of truth cannot lead anyone astray". In this epistemology, every truth claim pronounced by an individual is merely an opinion and may not necessarily be true for you as well.

Stemming from this epistemology comes a huge emphasis on emotions, which are commonly correlated with the heart. It follows that if the main way to find truth is to follow your heart, then emotions would be an expression of that truth that you have found. This is why in recent years there has been a huge push for emotional health and mental health, as this high view of emotions brings that to the surface. So much of our media and advertisements in the soil of postmodernism are targeted towards our emotions for us to feel something rather than logically deduce it with reason. Techniques such as bandwagon, having celebrities sell products, associating products with being cool or feeling a certain way, and the improvement of outward appeal on products are just some of the ways that this feeling-based soil has been promoted and marketed towards us.

With the elevated importance of emotions, however, comes some consequences, as it increases the chances of emotional damage and harassment. It also creates certain toxicity of conflicting interests that will be discussed in the bad fruits section of this chapter, but more on that later. Terms such as "snowflake" have been invented for a vast number of people who have been emotionally hurt and seem to snap at anything that disagrees with their emotions. Combined with the rise of social media in this soil, emotional damage and hurt have reached an all-time high. In a survey done in 2018, over 74% of people had felt so stressed that they felt overwhelmed or unable to cope with the stress. This was from a UK database with over 4,000 respondents [4].

This epistemology has crept into the religious sphere as well. A while ago, two missionaries from the Church of Jesus Christ of Latter-Day Saints came to my door (as is their main way of evangelism). I opened it gladly, as I have gained a certain love for these people because of my two years spent in a Mormon ministry at my college campus of Biola. I went into the conversation with an expectation of what they were going to say, as I have been in many interfaith dialogues before and am well versed in the LDS faith. How they responded to me saying I was an Evangelical Christian however, struck me as odd. After telling them my faith, they responded with the phrase "That's great! I'm glad you found a religion that works for you!". Reflecting on this interaction made me utterly confused. Did two missionaries, whose job for 2 years is to literally convert people to Mormonism, just say that I was ok believing whatever I already believed if it worked for me? It was interesting to see that relativism had even crept into the rigorously strict lives and teachings of the missionaries too. Evangelicals are not short on influence from relativism too, as one of the main things that thousands back their faith on is spiritual feelings and emotions. Not to discount these things as invalid, but it does represent a shift from the early church. Many of the earliest martyrs wouldn't have gone to the grave and picked up their cross for Christ on the basis of a simple spiritual feeling they had when praying. Many died for their beliefs because of the story of the historical Jesus and how they wanted to follow in his example. Emotions should still play a role in the Church today, as Jesus is one that engages both head and heart, but I think many have settled for only the latter.

The Good Fruit

The discussion of good and bad fruit of the postmodern soil is going to be a little bit different than all of the previous soils. This soil is very recent in its development and many of its major ideas stay as just ideas and are never really put into practice (at least in America). An example of this is the relativist ethics. While many say that they believe that ethics, good and evil are relative, they are quick to point out that something like the holocaust is terrible. It is hard to find the ideas of the postmodern soil put into consistent practice, as they like to spend most of their time floating around the cyberspace of Twitter and Facebook rather than in the physicality of everyday life. Many love to believe that their heart is the source of all truth, but they will still go to Google for answers. It is precisely this inconsistency that makes the good and bad fruits of the soil of postmodernism so hard to pinpoint. I have spent a fair amount of time searching for instances when postmodern thought led to physical oppression or a good thing, but the stories are few and far between.

The good fruit section then will be more of a praise for the movement, a sort of "what did the postmodern movement get right". The bad fruit section will act as a critique of postmodern thought and what some of the implications can be (if they were implemented at all in the United States) and have been when implemented in other countries. So, without further ado, here are some good things to come from the postmodern soil.

Increased Emphasis on Mental Health

I think that a great thing to come out of a time that focuses so much on emotions is the emphasis on emotional and mental health. This marks a big shift from past soils and in order to see this radical evolution in thought, we can look no further than the father of evolution himself, Charles Darwin. Quick side note, this is not a critique of *On the Origin of Species* or evolution, but on the effects of what that theory can do to the human psyche.

When Darwin first published his work *On the Origin of Species*, he had no idea or intention for the social implications that were to come from it. He was a firm naturalist and had not much interest in the social sphere or how his ideas would affect it. Of course, now we know just what damage the ideas of evolution, natural selection, and survival of the fittest have had on the social sphere in the early 1900s. Eugenics, the science of improving the genomic makeup of the human race, was a science stemming from Darwinian thought that was used to justify ethnic cleansing and the mass murdering of many racial minorities that were deemed impure. The sentiments of Darwinian thought when applied to society, also known as Social Darwinism, had reduced the human being, who a century before was glorified, to a mere vessel for the passing on of genetic information. As famous 20th-century French philosopher Jacques Monod puts it "The cell is a machine. The animal is a machine. Man is a machine".

The reduction of man to a mere machine in the early 1900s marked an all-time low for the awareness of the emotional and non-physical aspects of human existence. Many soldiers coming back from the World Wars received little to no mental counseling and a large number of soldiers developed PTSD and some even committed suicide because of the horrors they had seen. The soil of postmodernism does something better than the previous soils in that it focuses more on the emotional wellbeing of the individual. Sure, this does come at the expense of the limiting the glorification of reason and intelligence, but it is overall a good improvement to society and individuals. The human is now rarely viewed as a simple machine as it was in the early 1900s and the postmodern soil should receive some of the credit in bringing human dignity back to the forefront.

The effects of the increasing emphasis on mental health can be seen almost anywhere you go. On nearly every college campus, there are countless counselors, psychiatrists, nurses, and therapists that will help you through mental health issues. Many high schools and elementary schools even have a school psychiatrist or therapist that is available to meet with students. We even had "mental health Monday" at my high school where students would learn or participate in a certain activity such as yoga or breathing to improve mental health. Countless blogs and websites have popped up to help people control and manage stress and other emotional issues that have increased in our fast-paced society. There is even a National Institute of Mental Health that promotes and conducts extensive research on mental health and emotions.

This emphasis has allowed many people to live their lives with either less stress or ways to manage that stress practically. Mental health improvements have made millions of people's lives better in the day to day and have led to more insight into the complex human brain and emotions. This is undoubtedly one of the good fruits of the soil of postmodernism and is actually one of the only ideas of the movement that has been actualized in a way that is beneficial for society.

Expanded Voice

This next good fruit I am going to call "expanded voice". This is in reference to the expanding role that racial minorities and women have had in America and throughout Europe during the soil of postmodernism. Of course, this isn't perfect, as minorities are still underrepresented, but it does represent a major improvement over previous soils. There seems to be a correlation between the ideas of postmodernism and the increase in the number of people that are standing up for themselves and speaking out. It may be that the emphasis on emotions has driven them to speak, or maybe the reduction of truth to a subjective thing has given more confidence to the people in voicing their opinion. I don't really know the cause and I'm sure that you could do a lot of research and still know little about the cause of the expanded voice during this time.

The soil of postmodernism saw some of the biggest protests, marches, and social movements that have ever happened in America. It saw the rise of the Black Lives Matter movement, the Women's March, and the "Me Too" movement, just to name a few. While not everything about all of these movements could be called "good", there was a lot of progress made to expand the voice of minorities and their social wellbeing. These movements have gained a massive following and have helped communities come together and fight the injustices that we experience in our everyday lives.

Like many other of the postmodern ideas though, the expanded voice movements of the postmodern soil sort of just stop at that, an expanded voice. While the giant marches on D.C. for the Women's March gathered upwards of hundreds of thousands of people and raised millions of dollars, it largely didn't have an impact on policy, legislation, or appointed officials. Many protesters in the soil of postmodernism protest against something unjust, which is good, but nothing is then done to fix the injustice. The protests and expanded voice then, while good things, really didn't produce much good fruit for the human tree.

The one exception to this is the "Me too movement", which represents a bridge between this soil and the next. This movement actually made something happen and many injustices were exposed and made right by either imprisonment or destruction of public image. But overall, the good fruit of the postmodern soil has sold itself short. It would take yet another soil shift to make the semi-good fruits of the postmodern soil turn out for the better or in most cases the worse [5].

The Bad Fruits

Again, like the good fruits, the bad fruits are going to be hard to pinpoint because consistent postmodernism as an idea hasn't directly impacted many negative or positive events in a major way. It's not similar to the soil of technology, where we can clearly see the harmful effects of technology in the World Wars. Most of the bad events taking place during the postmodern soil were acts of terrorism and had nothing to do with the movement. Some bad ways of thinking, however, have begun to creep into our society and conversations on social media. This subtlety is what makes this soil just as dangerous in producing bad fruits as any of the other soils. The "bad fruit" of the soil of postmodernism then, will act more as a critique of these bad ideas and ways of thinking that have been and can be damaging to our society if implemented in the same way that many ideas were in previous soils.

The Robustness of the Worldview

The bad fruit of the soil of postmodernism is more of a weak fruit, or a defective fruit if we are continuing with the metaphor. This fruit is the lack of robustness of the postmodern worldview. To examine this, however, we must first give criteria that make a worldview robust.

I think that anyone could agree that the ten things I am about to propose as marks of a robust worldview are all good things and are worthy of the list. They are all things that every human long for and strives to achieve within their lifetime. Choosing a worldview that matches up with the most factors is desirable, and while others may come to different conclusions of what those factors are, I think that these ten should be included in the list. They even spell out the acrostic WORLDVIEWS, if you need any help remembering them.

W: Withstands logical suicide. This is first because if your worldview sets itself up for logical suicide then you don't have much to build off of and it is unlikely that it will be a robust worldview. If you are wondering what logical suicide is, it is just that, logic that kills itself simply by being stated. A statement such as "All statements are false" is a perfect example of this. It cannot be a true statement because if it was true, it would be false because it is itself a statement. Sorry if that got confusing, here is an easier example. The statement that I most commonly hear today is "it is wrong to say that anyone else is wrong". This is usually brought up in a discussion where you point out the flaws in someone else's worldview, religion, choice of sexuality, or anything else, you name it. Can you see how this statement kills itself though? By stating that it is wrong to say someone else is wrong, you just said that you think that their action was wrong in judging someone else. This point is probably the hardest to understand, but once you do it will help you to largely discern many of the self-defeating arguments that are so common in the public sphere today such as "we can't know the truth" or "every religion will get you to the truth".

O: Opens itself to rational scrutiny. This is an important one that I have seen so many worldviews fall short of in my lifetime. It is the idea that your worldview should not be isolated and make it illegal to hear other viewpoints. It should not be illegal to have doubts and to explore counterarguments or shy away from them. This is prevalent in the Mormon church as doubt is discouraged and for a long time, church documents were hidden and kept secret as to limit rational scrutiny. If a worldview cannot take rational scrutiny from others, then it is not robust and not worth investing your life into. Opposing viewpoints, in a worldview that is open to rational scrutiny, can actually help us grow and mature.

R: Resists the urge to downplay evil. It is a fact of this world that evil is out there. If you don't believe me, just turn on the news. Evil is a problem and therefore many worldviews have attempted to downplay its role in their belief system. It is a natural response because evil is so bad, and we want nothing to do with it. An example of this would be the alteration of the fall in Mormonism, or the pushing of evil onto gods in Greek pantheism. In Mormonism, the fall is celebrated because it gives us the ability to procreate and come to earth. In the ancient Greek religions, evil was thought of as a side effect of an angry god, that was arbitrarily annoyed. These examples are downplaying evil and the negative effects that it has on the world. A quick side note, I only use Mormonism in all of my examples because I know it best, not because I am bashing on them.

L: Lives well in everyday life. This is a hugely important part of a robust worldview because it involves how the worldview impacts the way you live and do your daily routine. If your worldview doesn't live well, then it isn't worth having because it stays merely in the intellectual space without being actualized. Some examples of this will be introduced in the next section, but a commonplace to turn is Marxism. This idea that everyone gets equal wealth and access to healthcare and basic needs sound great on paper. It does not, however, live well in everyday life as demonstrated in the mass death count that took place during the period of communism in the Soviet Union. Another worldview that doesn't live well in every day is hardcore naturalism, the view that everything is physical, and science can explain everything. In this view, held by famous Atheists such as Richard Dawkins, love is no more than the sum of a bunch of chemicals passing through synapses in your brain. But Dawkins' worldview doesn't live well in everyday life because he still goes home to his wife at night and says, "I love you", and I'm sure that he actually means it.

D: Deepens relational connections. A worldview shouldn't ostracize you from society and make you more isolated as an individual. Humans have a deep desire for relationships and that is because we were hardwired for them. In the famous book *Into the Wild* [6], the main character, Chris McCandless's worldview has him traveling the states as a hitchhiker in order to go and live in the

Alaskan wilderness. He eventually makes it to Alaska and lives in an abandoned bus for a few years before dying alone in the wilderness. At the end of his life, however, he comes to the powerful conclusion, scribbled in his notebook, "happiness best when shared". These four words captivate us because after reading the story through, we understand his point because we have felt the same sentiment. We desperately need relationships and a worldview that deepens them. There is a reason that solitary confinement is a punishment meant for the worst of criminals.

V: Vast explanatory power. A bad worldview takes a narrow way of seeing something and applies it to everything. A robust worldview grasps the complexity of life and seeks to explain it accordingly. No one simple thing should account for this complexity, as complex problems need complex solutions. A robust worldview doesn't stereotype people into categories or make blanket statements it can't support. It also must account for the basic needs of humanity to feel like they have a purpose and that they have dignity and respect. Historically, the lack of ability to explain the purpose of humanity during the post-war movement led to the vast nihilism and hopelessness that was prevalent during the latter half of the 20th century. A worldview should have answers to these questions.

I: Inspires artistic and scientific progress. Both science and art are extremely important to society as they are much of what makes up culture. If a worldview downplays these movements such as the destruction of art during the Nazi regime, it is not robust as it is not giving any progress to culture. Culture should be progressing and if your worldview does not encourage this progress then it may be doing more harm than good.

E: Engages both head and heart. As previously mentioned, the human being is not merely an intellectual person, but also has an emotional side that has been downplayed in the past with the onset of naturalism and reductionism. These worldviews had such a huge focus on the head, that they left out the heart, and many were swept away with hopelessness and were unable to enjoy the pleasures of this world. Some worldviews have overemphasized the heart so much that they lose the head.

In Buddhism for example, the ultimate goal of life is to achieve Nirvana, a state of complete nothingness. To do this, you must completely control your emotions and yourself through meditation. In this process, you repeat mantras, which are silly little phrases that are meant to clear your brain and enter you into a state of mindlessness. You must first lose your mind to reach enlightenment. It is similar in Hinduism, where gurus can be seen taking copious amounts of drugs and marijuana in order to enter themselves into a mindless state, in order to reach enlightenment. A robust worldview should not sacrifice head nor heart and should engage both to produce wholistic human beings.

W: Worldview aware beyond its own borders. This is similar to receiving scrutiny but is still another important component to a robust worldview. This component is more concerned with how the openness of your worldview engages in day-to-day conversations and interactions. A robust worldview doesn't just learn the straw-man versions of every other worldview to crush it in a debate but takes the time to learn what real people believe and act out in their life. A good example of this comes from a recent trip I took to Utah to have interfaith dialogues. Going into the trip, learning about Mormon doctrine and beliefs, it is easy to have a fantasized version of the Mormon worldview and assume that everyone who believes this stuff is either crazy or delusional. In our interactions, however, our presuppositions were changed as these people were smart individuals who even didn't agree with some of the things that we had been taught Mormons believe. You must always take the time to learn someone's worldview from them directly rather than assuming you know it already to be worldview aware. Dostoyevsky, in my opinion, does this better than I have seen among any other writer. In his books, he puts his main characters up against iron giants, people with opposing worldviews that are represented with extremely convincing and strong arguments. This can be most clearly seen in *Crime and Punishment*, where the main character, Raskolnikov, is given a complex decision. To give a little background, his sister is in an abusive relationship in order to provide the poor family with wealth, and the story presents us with a rich pawn broker that Raskolnikov interacts with whom is a horrible person that everyone hates and who also abuses his niece on the daily. Raskolnikov is then given a very tough decision. He could kill the apparently terrible pawn broker and take his wealth, which would free his sister from the abusive relationship as well as the pawn broker's niece, or he could just let all the injustice happen. Can you see how good of a case Dostoyevsky makes for murder? In all of his books, no straw man argument is presented, and every situation is as complex as the real world requires it to be. I think that we can all learn from Dostoyevsky in this aspect.

S: Spurs just social action. A robust worldview should not be one that just stays in your head but causes you to do something about the injustices in the world. A worldview that is passive against such things is not robust and does not do much good for society. It should be noted, however, that not all social action is good, as there are plenty of social movements such as racial segregation and Hitler's Kristallnacht that are not good. By social action, I am talking about the good kind obviously, as a worldview that provokes bad social action is probably not a good choice. Many worldviews in the past have championed this attribute and have done much to eliminate the injustices of this world. The Christian worldviews of Martin Luther King Jr. and William Wilberforce led them to fight for civil rights in America and abolish slavery in England. The worldview of many enlightenment thinkers led to the expansion of the social sphere and democracy throughout Europe and the Americas. A robust worldview always leads to social action because all ideas have real-world implications.

So How Does a Postmodern Worldview Match Up?

After learning the ten things that make a worldview robust, we must now apply these things to the postmodern worldview to see how it matches or fails to match many of the categories. Hopefully, this analysis will be insightful for understanding modern sentiments of postmodern thought and how it is playing out in the lives of those who believe it.

W: Withstands logical suicide. One of the central absolute truths of the postmodern movement is that "there is no absolute truth" and "all truth is relative". Can you see what is wrong with that statement already? It has claimed to be an "absolute truth" although if it is true, then it is also false because there is no "absolute truth". The very foundations of postmodernism commit logical suicide. You also hear many postmodern thinkers saying things like "don't judge" or "you shouldn't force your beliefs on others". These do not withstand logical suicide as the statement "don't judge" is in fact judging and "don't force your beliefs on others" is forcing a belief on another. I could keep going with these statements, but I think the point is made that it does not withstand logical suicide.

O: Opens itself to rational scrutiny. This category is a hard one to pin down for the postmodern movement because, while most are open to scrutiny and hearing other beliefs, they ultimately dismiss all of them with the phrase "it may be true for you, but not for me". This presupposition about truth is what makes postmodernism almost immune from rational scrutiny because any argument made against the worldview can simply be dismissed in the same way. Whenever someone is giving a truth claim, through a postmodern lens, they are merely stating their opinion. Therefore, for the majority of people in the postmodern soil, they are not open to rational scrutiny.

R: Resists the urge to downplay evil. One of the hardest questions that the postmodernist has to deal with is the problem of evil. In order to be consistent with their worldview, they cannot universally categorize what is evil because that would be an absolute truth. They can barely make value judgments at all about what is evil or what is good because all truth is merely their opinion. They cannot consistently say "The mass killings committed by Stalin and Mao did during their communist regimes is evil" and must rather settle for the unsettling, "I think that the mass killings of Stalin and Mao in their communist regimes is evil, but that is just my opinion". The banner of tolerance gives you no ground to concretely name things as evil. The evil of child sacrifice practiced by certain native tribes in Africa becomes a "valuable cultural tradition", the Holocaust becomes a "way that Hitler decided to run his country" and terrorism is just "people exercising their freedoms". Pastor and Theologian John Piper put these sentiments best on one of his episodes of the Desiring God Podcast [7].

"For example, suppose you are a professor in a university and you have absorbed a postmodern mindset that playfully says, "What is right for you is right for you and what is right for me is right for me and what is wrong for you is wrong for you and what is wrong for me is wrong for me and we don't impose our morality on each other. There is no one absolute right and wrong, good and bad, beautiful and ugly." The truth gets squashed down onto our perceptions and preferences. That is just rampant, right? That is just rampant. And it is playful, and it is going to come to an end when that professor walks into a real living holocaust himself. So whatever the situation is, he walks into an experience of 6 million Jewish people murdered, or 60 million under the Stalinist regime starved and killed in the Gulags, or we are remembering 100 years this year since the Armenian genocide of the Turkish people slaughtering a million and a half Armenians between Turkey and Syria in 1915. You walk into that as a professor who has been playing word games on tenure with students, fitting them to be destroyed by the world in which they live with this absolute nonsense that, "What is right for you is right for you and what is wrong for me is wrong for me." And suddenly he is so confronted by evil, he finds welling up out of his heart a statement he thought would never come. "That is evil."

L: Lives well in everyday life. As we have seen already, postmodern ideas look great on paper but don't really work out too well in everyday life. On college campuses, many postmodern students are also closely associated with the desire of a socialist country. A recent survey has found that nearly one-half of millennials are receptive of living under socialism. Socialism, don't get me wrong, looks great on paper. Poverty would be almost abolished, everyone would get the healthcare and basic needs met, there aren't oppressive companies and rich citizens taking our money, and there is no more inequality. But how does it actually work out in real life? For this, we will have to dive into the socialist experiments of Stalin's Russia, Chavez-Maduro's Venezuela, Mao's China, and Hitler's Germany. The horrors that all of these countries have produced is too much to write about in this small book. After visiting the Soviet Union, the French Nobel Laureate writer Andre Gide said: "I doubt at any time in any country in the world – not even in Hitler's Germany – have the mind and spirit ever been less free, more bent, more terrorized and indeed visualized than in the Soviet Union.". The Chinese philosopher Lin Yutang listed the "little terrors" that prevailed in China – making children of 12 subject to capital punishment, sending women to work in underground coal mines, and harassing workers during their lunchtime with threats of prison if they were late returning to work. In Venezuela, over 6 million hectares were robbed from owners of local farms and food production fell 75% in the socialist regime. It went from being the wealthiest South American country to one of the poorest. In 1999, the Stéphane Courtois introduction to the *Black Book of Communism* [8] gave a "rough approximation, based on unofficial estimates" approaching 100 million killed under the regime of socialism. It is easy to see how this does not live well in everyday life.

D: Deepens relational connections. A big factor in deep relational connections is a shared value in conviction or belief. For example, two Christians could become friends over their shared views of life and convictions in the truth of scripture. Such deep connections are inherently destroyed in the postmodern worldview because of how it handles truth. Instead of unifying people under a banner of truth, it utterly disunifies people by reducing truth to opinion. People are no longer united with common beliefs because ultimately, your beliefs are only true for you. This severely isolates people because one of the basic desires of human life is to be a part of something bigger than themselves. This is something that is lost when you throw away all metanarratives in a postmodern worldview and by saying that there is no truth that is outside of your subjective experience.

V: Vast explanatory power. As we saw with the problem of evil, postmodernism lacks explanatory power. It struggles with explaining evil, it is hard to know what is beautiful, or even what is good. Another hallmark of postmodern thought is a stereotyping and tribal thinking patterns associated with Marxist ideas. In Marx's *Communist Manifesto*, he presents the idea of class struggle, and that everything wrong with society can be boiled down to corrupt systems. This is an extremely narrow view of people and society, and cannot explain the complex problems of everyday life. In this mindset, everyone who disagrees with you or is causing evil in the world can be described as one letter in the TRIBES acrostic. You are either a theocrat, a racist, an islamophobe, a bigot, an elitist, or a sexist. This narrow view of people is extremely damaging as we will soon see in the next soil and lacks the complexity needed for a robust worldview.

I: Inspires artistic and scientific progress. A while ago, I visited the modern art museum in Philadelphia. The outside of the building itself was a masterpiece of art, so I expected nothing less from the art exhibits. I was half correct in assuming this. Many of the exhibits were quite nice and had great art, but one exhibit, in particular, didn't. This "modern art" exhibit displayed a urinal on the wall, with nothing written on it, as a piece of art. According to the postmodern narrative, I should expect this. Art has become subjective as beauty is in the eye of the beholder. With this in mind, art can be literally anything, which I am not sure if I can call progress given my experience with the urinal. Scientific progress suffers similarly. While most postmodernists aren't opposed to science and even take to heart the struggles of climate change and other scientific problems of the day, this is very inconsistent with their worldview. Science is the pursuit of truth; it is finding out object things about the universe. This is in direct opposition to a worldview that states "all truth is relative" and "there is no such thing as absolute truth". Scientific education then isn't a way to learn objective truth, but a way to get indoctrinated into believing someone else's truth claims. If there is no such thing as capital "T" truth, then education in the sciences becomes useless. Higher education becomes either a diploma printing mill or just propaganda to make young adults believe whatever the older generation wants it to. By championing tolerance, the postmodernist must accept all types of scientific ideas, even ones that deserve better examination and ethical caution such as eugenics, embryo editing, and cloning. I think that in general, consistent postmodernism does not promote good science or art.

E: Engages both head and heart. Much of what can be said on this topic stems from the paragraph above, as it is clear to see that this worldview does not put much emphasis on the head by eliminating objective truth. The heart, however, receives the majority of the emphasis as you may have realized from reading the chapter thus far. All of the "cool" communication of our day revolves around getting you to feel something in that ten-second advertisement with the cute puppy, or that poster of the Nike shoe being worn by your favorite basketball player. Nobody, except for maybe the scientists, are showing you the intricate statistics and exact ingredients in order to sell their product or get you to believe their story, they are turning to experience. "How does it make you feel?" or "This product will deepen your peace and rest" are common phrases used in this age of cool communication that drives right at your heart. If you have ever seen a commercial for a fast-food restaurant, you will understand what I mean. No fast food restaurant is trying to sell you their Big Mac or Whopper by stating the facts on how healthy it is, or how much protein it has. They sell their product by showing you a nice video of them grilling the burger, slapping the lettuce on there just right, the juice squirting out of the tomato as they cut it, and the slo-mo of a really happy person taking a bite and giving a big smile. As you can probably tell, this form of advertising is very engaging to the heart, heck, even I'm craving a fast-food hamburger right now writing this! So, as a final consensus, no, I do not think that the postmodern worldview engages both the head and heart well, as it only focuses on the latter.

W: Worldview aware beyond its own borders. This is the first place where I think that the postmodern worldview holds up pretty nicely and does a fine job. Many in the movement are extremely aware of other worldviews because they are usually people who have come from other worldviews (of course, after determining that all of them are true even though they contradict each other). Many "worldview hoppers" end up becoming either atheists, with no hope in a higher being, or some form of postmodernist, who affirms all religions as true. Much of the mass media involved in the postmodern movement such as BuzzFeed, is extremely worldview aware. There are episodes where they will have Christians on, Muslims, Atheists, or even devil worshipers. This does a good thing in exposing people to a diverse set of worldviews that one may not receive in their own tradition.

S: Spurs just social action. It is hard to address the issue of social action with a postmodernist because many are inconsistent as we saw when it came to the problem of evil and what is good. I think that so many people in the postmodern soil are propelled into social action with great numbers based on their idea of tolerance, which is a good thing. This, however, doesn't match up well with the lack of standards by which to judge good and evil in the world. A consistent postmodernist would have no grounds for social justice because there are no grounds for condemning evil. Evil to a postmodernist isn't something objective, it is just a cultural expression that we have no responsibility in judging. It is extremely hard to find a consistent postmodernist that ignores good and evil in the world because they would be the most hated person on the planet. Relativist morality in theory cuts off cross-cultural examination and does not allow us to stop horrible actions being taken in other countries. Without an objective view of right and wrong, we would have no business judging the human trafficking and slavery that still exists in many parts of the world today or even the corrupt communist countries that kill and abuse citizens. Social progress always comes from absolutists, people that believe that the world can be objectively better and that there is a real definition of good and evil. People like William Wilberforce, who abolished slavery in England, did so because he felt a conviction in his heart that slavery was evil, and he was opposed to evil. By a postmodern lens, what he did was intolerant of the English belief that slavery was good for the economy. It was a bad thing for Wilberforce to "judge" the standards of the day and to introduce new standards of living that contradicted the old. Without the work of absolutists in this world, social justice and action wouldn't be possible. Social action does not flow freely from a postmodern worldview.

A Final analysis of the soil of postmodernism

We now come to the end of an extensive critique of the postmodern soil. You may have noticed that more ink was spilled in this chapter than any thus far and this is not without a purpose. I believe that this soil is the most important to understand because it is relevant to understanding the current sentiments of today as well as where we are headed. Hopefully, it was helpful to closely examine the ins and outs and practical implications that the soil has had on society and in the lives of those who buy into its precepts. There is still one more story I do want to tell, however. It may seem strange and even quite ironic because it is a story that comes from a Disney movie, which I have gone to lengths to show propagates the postmodern message. But this one is different.

In the first *Incredibles* movie, we are introduced to the main villain in his earlier years, Buddy, or as he will later be called, Syndrome. He desperately wants the attention of Mr. Incredible and follows everything he says in hopes of joining him on his mission. He is met with disappointment however, as Mr. Incredible barely even acknowledges his existence. After experiencing this disillusionment with Mr. Incredible, Buddy says an astonishing phrase to include in a Disney movie: "You always told me to be true to myself, but you never told me which part of myself to be true to". Buddy had been fed the postmodern sentiment of "be true to yourself" [9] by Mr. Incredible, but he was left in confusion after realizing that he is in fact two selves. There is an evil side and a good side to everyone as he soon realizes, and when we see him later in the movie, he has followed the evil side of himself and ends up as the main antagonist Syndrome. In this situation, you almost feel bad for Syndrome as he was just a by-product of the destructiveness of postmodern thought. It may seem like the phrase "be true to yourself is great advice", but in reality, it leaves people confused and hopeless as they don't know which part of themselves to be true to.

This is precisely the sentiment that is causing the human tree to begin to be uprooted from the soil of postmodernism. People are tired of the confusion that comes from relative morality and shallow phrases such as "be true to yourself". People are starting to become bored with trying to "find their own meaning" and "follow their heart" to no success. All these factors and more are causing a shift in the soil in America and throughout Europe away from the postmodern mindset. People are gravitating towards absolutes because they are starving for meaning and purpose in their life. Cult membership is at an all-time high and political participation has become a religion. This is the uprooting that is taking over the news of 2019 and 2020: the soil of polarization.

8

THE SOIL OF POLARIZATION

We now enter our current soil (At least the one of 2019-2020. I'm not sure when you are reading this). Almost everyone in this soil has latched onto something to be a part of. People are no longer accepting any opinion as valid but are in fact hyperjudgmental of just about every word that comes out of peoples' mouths on social media. The mantra is no longer "follow your heart" but is "follow the Democratic party" or "follow the Republican party". There is no more sentiment of "your truth is your truth" as many are labeled bigot, racist, or privileged for holding a certain view. Tolerance has been replaced with political correctness and the epistemology has changed from following your own heart to following that of social media and your party of choice. It is truly a soil of polarization and a shift towards a more authoritarian view of life that was not seen in the soil of postmodernism. In the soil of polarization, there are absolutes, but if you disagree with them, you are hated and bullied until you agree. This is our current soil.

So how did the human tree get to where it is today? How did we become obsessed with politics and joining causes bigger than ourselves? I think in part it came from the lack of basic needs being met during the soil of postmodernism. Humans all have a desire to worship something or someone, be in a community, deal with guilt and shame that enters into our lives, and to seek meaning that is bigger than ourselves. These basic human desires were not being met during the soil of postmodernism because worshiping yourself became boring, being true to yourself became isolating, removing objective morality made it hard to even define guilt and shame, and following your heart led you down a path of emptiness because it was too small a meaning. The human tree got tired of its needs not being met, so the soil started to shift. Authoritarian structures such as political parties happen to meet these desires quite well. The political party becomes a figure of worship, you enter into a community with likeminded political allies who support all of your ideas, you can project your guilt and shame onto the opponent and corrupt systems, and you can find meaning in protests, the political party agenda, and winning elections.

If you remember the historical cycle we explored in the chapter on the postmodern soil, then you will have noticed that the "cycle" didn't really cycle and just ended in postmodernism. This is because the last step, as the first in the cycle, is an authoritarian rule. The cycle began with the authority of religion, which slowly lost authoritative power and the dominant worldview became one where you were the authority of your own life. This cycle comes full circle, however, as it has come to the soil of polarization, a very authoritarian society with the authority being politics rather than religion.

American journalist Sydney J. Harris said that "History repeats itself, but in such cunning disguise that we never detect the resemblance until the damage is done". This sentiment could not be truer of the soil of polarization, as it shares many characteristics with the soil of religion. Like the religious soil, people appeal to political parties and their favorite news source to find truth. Like the Roman Catholic Church, power is the ultimate goal of society and everyone is in a competition for more of it. Like the religious systems of indulgences and relics, there are many institutions today that present some of the same injustices and burdens on citizens. We can learn a lot about our current soil through historical reflection and education. An important step in healing the wounds that our current soil has caused is to look back. Go study the protestant reformation and how they radically opposed the injustices of the authority of the day. Go read about William Wilberforce and how he went against the status quo to crush slavery in England. Go read about John Newton, and his radical opposition to the Trans-Atlantic Slave Trade. By reflecting on these people and movements, I promise you will gain a greater insight into our current age because it is so similar in form.

To further understand how we got here, we can take a cue from psychology, in particular the psychology of cults. When answering the question "Who joins cults?" [1] Robert Schecter and Margaret Singer, both researchers from the American Family Foundation, found that it wasn't the impoverished kids that were joining cults. It was actually the middle-class citizen who was lonely, depressed, and in search of deeper meaning in life. They found that one of the largest recruiting areas is college campuses, where students are free from the authoritarian rule of their parents. Understanding this study can help inform us why the soil is shifting from postmodernism. People are joining cults and latching onto authority because that is what people were designed to do and they have been deprived of it for the past 20 years of the postmodern soil. This is why children who are raised under very loose conditions are more likely to latch onto a cult because they desperately desire something bigger than themselves to latch onto.

Defining Characteristics of the soil

We haven't had a section like this in previous soils, or maybe we have but it was never explicitly named. I think this is because this particular soil is the most confusing. It is confusing because the epistemology is more difficult to pinpoint, human to human interactions seem to talk past each other in vain, and many times the truth is lost in a flutter of political interpretations and implications of that truth. Therefore, it is important to accurately define this soil so that we may be cautious of the things about it that are harmful and damaging to the soul and lives of others.

Where Does Truth Come From?

In the postmodern soil, truth was relative and came from your emotions. In the soil of polarization, truth comes mainly from social media, in particular, social media that supports your political viewpoint. Whenever a major event happens nowadays, there are thousands of news stories that come out, each with their own political lens and bias infused into the article. It becomes so easy for people to parous around social media and select an article that fits with their viewpoint and then repost it without even attempting to read the articles that disagree with his or her political stance. This can be almost more damaging than finding truth in yourselves like in the postmodern soil because at least there you aren't in raging opposition to the opponent. So often, social media battles go like this.

Person 1: "Look at this article. It is very informative and a great read. X is such a great person and his work with Y project is phenomenal."

Person 2: "You should really check your privilege and racism. Look at all the terrible things X has done and here is an article to prove it."

Person 1: "People like you who post these articles are just narrow-minded bigots that blindly support X political party. The things in that article are very untrue and misleading."

Person 2: "You have no power to talk on this subject because you are a straight white male who doesn't understand the struggles of others. Read this article."

You can see how this would be confusing and destructive. Truth is easier than ever to mutate and change to whatever you want it to be, which is a dangerous thing for an epistemology. For a source of truth to be firm in its foundations, it shouldn't be able to mutate to whatever you want and should be telling objective facts about reality. The truth is that it is really hard to find the truth amidst the clatter of opinions about the truth, and many people just don't have time to take up that search. People are quick to judge but slow to listen. Quick to accept something as true from their viewpoint, but also quick to dismiss anything that doesn't agree with them. This destructive method of seeking truth is not helped by social media, as the only articles you are going to see are the ones that your friends are sharing, and your friends are more likely to share your viewpoints. It has all too easily created a polarizing society in which the people in the middle are forced to pick a side or become destroyed in the crossfire. If three words could describe the soil, it would be "Us vs. Them".

How do We Act Towards Ideological Opponents?

In the postmodern soil, the banner of tolerance was waved vigorously, and if you disagreed with this banner, you were intolerant. The labeling of people and mass stereotyping of the postmodern soil has carried over into the polarizing soil to a greater extreme. If you disagree with a sentiment posted on social media, the TRIBES mentality comes to the forefront once again. I have seen too many posts after a tragedy saying things such as "all white people are privileged and need to check their privilege… if you don't agree you are racist and are part of the problem", "If you don't stand up with us and repost this, you are adding to the problem and are sexist", and "Christians are the problem with this world and they are narrow-minded and disrespectful to think they can go to church during the virus". While many of these sentiments aren't bad in themselves, there is a destructive way of thinking that is behind them. It usually goes like this: one individual of a group will do something terrible, and then this will get blown way out of proportions and used as a banner by which to judge the entire group based on previous hatred towards them. Take the recent example of churches in California, which as of the writing of this book are still shut down due to COVID-19. [4] A few of these churches, most prominently John MacArthur's church and a few Calvary Chapels, opened against government orders and in my opinion, rightly so. The amount of bullying and hateful coverage from both the government and the media was outrageous, as officials even threatened to cut power to these churches. The media and governments who already hated the Church and God had finally found another missile to launch an attack on the church in this incident. Statements such as "see, look at how ignorant Christians are" and "Christians are one of the main problems" have come out of countless numbers of social media posts about the topic and have attempted to paint a picture of the Church as a defiant and harmful organization. This harmful grouping of people and stereotyping can also be seen in the socialist argument, the modern Black Lives Matter movement, and is especially prevalent whenever Democrats or Republicans are mentioned. Blanket statements have become the most common and easiest way to dismiss the opinions of entire people groups without giving their ideas much scrutiny. Everything is politicized and there is no room in the public sphere to wrestle with complex issues as people once did in the enlightenment era. Issues must now be handled immediately, and you must take a side or else you are just "being silent and contributing to the problem" [2]. One way that people attempt to do this is by claiming something as "science". Many think that once something enters the realm of science, it is a fact. Being a scientist, I can tell you this is far from the truth. People will take hotly debated political issues such as abortion and make it a scientific issue to silence opponents. This practice has become even more prevalent with the outbreak of COVID-19 and continues to rampage through popular media, producing a pile of conflicting facts and double standards.

One of the major drivers behind the toxic view of the opponent is the radical deconstructionism that has taken foot in our modern society. This is the sentiment that there is a secret bias or meaning behind every argument and it is your job to "deconstruct" that bias from their argument. One of the greatest deconstructionist mantras of the modern soil is expressed in the phrase "Everything is masking power". Through this lens, every post you make about how abortion is wrong is just you masking your male Christian power, every post about how great Trump is or isn't is simply a power move against blacks or Hispanics, and every post about how events in the news are blown out of proportions is an attempt to increase the power of your political party. The main question that is being asked about news articles, social media posts, and other sources of media isn't "Is this true?" but rather, "how are you protecting your power or privilege by posting this?". People are madly in love with deconstructing "deeper meanings" from posts that had no intended deeper meaning at all. This is an extremely damaging thing and one of the major factors into why I've called this soil the soil of polarization. The moment one person starts to deconstruct the bias of the other, the two begin to talk past each other and never really address the main point of the post or issue at all. Person 1 may link an article that analyzes the complexities of systemic racism and how blanket statements shouldn't be made, and then Person 2 will come along and say that Person 1 is protecting his privilege by not agreeing with his/her viewpoint and is ignorant to the issue. Person 1 must now respond to Person 2 by explaining how he isn't ignorant and racist and seeking the protection of his own privilege. And after hours upon hours of back and forth between Person 1 and 2, they have neglected to have a real conversation about the issue at hand, an issue that requires extensive and civil debate and discussion. You can see this type of thinking and acting most apparently in the political debates. Presidential candidates no longer answer the questions asked of them with civility and truthfulness but instead slam insult after insult at the other candidate in hopes to degrade their appeal to the public. These candidates are simply talking past the main issues and settling for disagreements that can be found in a children's schoolyard.

To drive this point home, a recent example must be invoked. Fairly recently to the publication of this book, there was another resurgence of the Black Lives Matter movement after the horrible and unjust death of George Floyd. If you don't remember this, then you must've been hiding in a cave during that time because it was literally everywhere on every social platform. In the midst of social media posts condemning racism and injustice, many Christians took to the platforms to demonstrate the fact that "all lives matter" rather than going with the popular movement of "black lives matter". While I see their flaw in posting this and missing the very core message of the Black Lives Matter movement, the backlash against these innocent posters was what worried me most. While I must admit, not all of the backlash was bad and some sources were open to civil correction and discussion, the vast majority of the backlash represented this very deconstructionism that is so common in the soil of polarization. Many posts against "all lives matter" accused the people of posting it of "protecting their privilege" and "giving an excuse to protect their power as a white citizen". They assumed that the people who post "all lives matter" don't actually care about black lives and won't address the actual racism in the country (and then proceeded to throw in Luke 15:3-7 out of context). These are lofty things to assume of a person and I would bet that if you polled all of the Christians who posted it that the vast majority would agree that racism towards blacks is evil and that blacks are seen equally in God's eyes. By assuming their motives, a toxic environment founded on hate, not love, has been created, and disunity, not unity has been formed.

The real danger behind deconstructionism is that you are claiming to know and understand the intentions and the heart of the person you are deconstructing. This is an impossible task for any mere human, as Biblically, it is a task left for God and God alone. Jesus was the only man to ever fully know the thoughts and intentions of man and what their "true motivation" is in the heart. This was because he was God. We see this throughout the scriptures.

Yet, O Lord of hosts, You who test the righteous,

Who see the mind and the heart;

Let me see Your vengeance on them;

For to You I have set forth my cause. – Jeremiah 20:12

And knowing **their thoughts** Jesus said to them, "Any kingdom divided against itself is laid waste; and any city or house divided against itself will not stand. – Matthew 12:25

But **Jesus perceived their malice**, and said, "Why are you testing Me, you hypocrites? – Matthew 22:18

But **He knew what they were thinking**, and He said to the man with the withered hand, "Get up and come forward!" And he got up and came forward. – Luke 6:8

And God, **who knows the heart**, testified to them giving them the Holy Spirit, just as He also did to us; - Acts 15:8

Anyone claiming to also know this information is claiming to perform a task that only God can do and is, therefore, claiming to be God themselves. I hope that if anything, this section has begun to expose you to the dangers of deconstructionism and claiming to "know" the intentions of others. I hope that it will begin to change the way you approach complex issues and debate that conforms more in lines of the loving and truth-seeking ways of Jesus.

To pin the nail in the coffin, one of my favorite theologians, Thaddeus Williams, who I have had the great privilege of being a student of, has this to say on the modern deconstructive conversation climate:

"Conversations about social justice in our polarized age tend to generate more heat than light because of a phenomenon we may call "the Newman Effect." In 2018 Canadian psychology professor Jordan Peterson joined BBC Channel 4 host Cathy Newman to discuss gender inequality in what became one of the most viral interviews of the 21st century. The lively exchange sparked the famous "So you're saying" meme, based on Newman's repeated use of that phrase to interpret Peterson's statements in the most unflattering and inflammatory light possible.
"You're saying that women want to dominate…"
"So, you're saying that anyone who believes in equality… should basically give up, because it ain't gonna happen.…

You're saying that's fine. The patriarchal system is just fine…"

"You're saying that women are not intelligent enough to run these top companies…"

"You're saying that Transactivists could lead to the deaths of millions of people…"

"You're saying that we should organize our societies along the lines of the lobsters…"

Professor Peterson, of course, wasn't saying any of that. His perspective did not fit neatly into the black-and-white boxes of our day, so anything that seemed out-of-synch with Newman's perspective was taken in the most extreme, cartoonish, and damning way possible.

The truth is, we are all Cathy Newmans now, and that has become a serious existential threat to the unity of the church. "Racism is still a problem." "So, you're saying we should abandon the Gospel and embrace neo-Marxism." "Black lives matter." "So, you're saying all lives don't matter." "The fact that over 70 percent of black children are born without two parents in the home should matter to us." "So, you're saying you're a racist, blaming the victim, and saying the black community's problems are completely their own fault." "Marriage is a complementary union between a male and a female." "So, you're saying you hate gay people." "During the Covid-19 pandemic, we should shelter in place to protect the most vulnerable." "So, you're saying you are anti-freedom and want us all to bow to tyranny." "We should re-open the economy to help those whose livelihoods and mental health are being devastated by quarantine." "So, you're saying you want the virus to spread and more people to die." The list could go on and on.

This is what conversations about important questions have reduced to in our day and age. The only way someone could possibly disagree with me is if they are a bad person, a sworn enemy of justice. And so we tar-and-feather any dissonant idea with the absolute worst ideologies we can imagine. The result is rampant self-righteousness, a loss of humble self-criticism, widespread confirmation bias, a loss of real listening required to reach nuanced truths, and pervasive partisanship, a loss of real community that requires us to give charity and the benefit of the doubt to others. As Christians, let's do better."

As we saw in the postmodern soil, evil was such an abstract thing that it was impossible to categorize or judge. Outrage against injustice could just be brushed off as chatter in the wind or a mere opinion that evil is bad. This thought pattern shifts dramatically in the soil of polarization. Evil has gone from something that is extremely abstract, to something very concrete and almost exclusively so. If you asked someone in the postmodern soil to point out evil, they'd have difficulty, but someone in this modern soil would guide you directly to it and even give you 10 things you can try to do to stop that so-called evil. Why is this? It is because evil in the soil of polarization is said to lie in the corrupt systems and institutions. It is a "systemic" thing to use some of the current terminologies and has deep roots in systems and history. In this view, evil is some sort of built-in component of many (Western) societies and can be done away with through the elimination of the corrupt systems, through policy reform, and protests.

For example, let's look at the evil of modern-day racism. I cannot count the number of times even in the past week that I have heard "Racism is a systemic evil and here are 10 ways to counter the system". While I do agree that racism is an evil [3] that has been around for a very long time in the United States, it is wishful thinking that destroying the system will actually destroy the evil. In fact, much if not all of the systemically racist institutions in the United States such as Redlining, Jim Crow, segregation, the ability to vote, etc., have already been destroyed, yet racism still exists. Even if all racist policies and institutions are burned at the stake, racism will still exist because racism isn't a system problem, it is a sin problem.

A further example can be found in modern-day slavery. Nobody is talking much about this nowadays, but it is very much still a huge problem even in the United States. I don't think people talk about it because it demonstrates the failure of their systemic evil narrative. Slavery as a system has been abolished in the United States and openly condemned since June of 1865 when the emancipation proclamation was signed. But it still exists. After the destruction of the main institution of evil, which was the Trans-Atlantic Slave Trade and the legality of slavery in the United States, more evil institutions popped up. It is as though evil is a hydra, you cut off one head and two grow back in its place. In this case, a major victory was won in cutting off the head of "legal slavery", but what grew in its place was the disguised slavery in the pornography industry and the coercion of impoverished people to slavery. So now what do we do? We had seemingly done everything right and had defeated the evil institution and system, but the problem didn't go away. This is where the current narrative breaks down.

What then do people say when their efforts to beat the system fail such as it is with racism right now. The civil rights movement of the 1960s tackled the issue of racism and segregation and for the most part, accomplished its goal of expanding rights to blacks and ending segregation. But after the civil rights movement seemingly defeated the system, we still have racism and segregation. So, what happened? The current fighters of racism will tell you that "we still haven't done enough to fight the deep issues of racism in America". It seems that no matter how many institutional and systemic victories are won, the problem is still deeper down and has not been won yet.

I think there is a better way. Why not, instead of trying to defeat systems on the outside, we hit the problem directly at its core, penetrating to the deep problem that is the at the bottom of racism, sexism, intolerance, slavery, homicide, violent crime, sexual assault, police brutality, pride, and injustice. This we will soon explore.

9

THE PROBLEM AT THE ROOTS

We have now reached the end of our long and quite unsatisfying journey throughout time, so I think it is important that I recap where we have been. The human tree began in the soil of religion and stayed there for quite some while (I guess the world moves much faster today. Maybe it is the consumer mindset.). This soil caused the human tree to produce a lot of good fruits: universities began to spring up, the renaissance brought beautiful artwork and sculptures to Europe, and the scientific revolution quite literally revolutionized science and the way we viewed the world. The soil wasn't perfect though and produced many bad fruits as well such as religious crusades, corruption within the church, and a brutal enslavement and conversion process of the Native Americans.

In order to try and find a way to eliminate the bad fruit, the human tree uprooted itself from religion and replanted in the soil of secularism, the Godless soil. At first, this soil produced a lot of good fruit for the human tree such as the enlightenment's emphasis on reason and logic, and humanism's elevation of the view of man. These good fruits were not long last, however, and the championing of reason soon accompanied mass murder of innocent civilians as well as the enslavement and oppression of others who were deemed "less human".

This bad fruit caused the human tree to look elsewhere for a soil that would produce good fruit, so it was planted in the soil of technology and innovation. Much good fruit came from this soil such as innovations that change how we live today like the automobile, steam engine, and airplane. This technology also raised the standard of living for many citizens, bringing them out of life on the farm as sharecroppers and into the factories to earn a decent wage. This soil, like the others though, failed to avoid producing bad fruits. The technology meant for the advancement of human society caused two world wars that drastically set back human progress in many ways. The factories also mistreated children and caused them to work dangerous jobs with little pay.

The devastation of the wars caused the human tree to turn quickly towards something more peaceful, the soil of love and peace. Set upon the great foundations of love and peace, it would seem like this soil could only produce good fruit, but this was not the case. While it did produce tight-knit communities and quite successful anti-war protests, the soil also made space for one of the greatest drug addictions and abuses of relationships among its members.

The human tree was then replanted into the soil of economics and saw great fruit almost immediately. The economy was booming, and more and more citizens were entering the middle class and being able to live comfortable lives in the American dream. With the prosperity at home, however, came corruption and abject poverty in other countries with which the US was involved within Latin America. Dictatorships were supported to fight communism, and many democratically elected presidents were assassinated or removed from office by the US either directly or indirectly through funding revolutions. There was also a lot of internal corruption within the presidency and big businesses with Watergate being the poster boy for this.

All of these factors led many Americans to gain a distaste for big businesses and our economy, so the human tree was replanted in the soil of postmodernism. This soil had some positive aspects and good fruit for the human tree such as an expanded democratic voice and increased awareness of emotional health. It seemed like this would be the ideal soil because making truth subjective doesn't give you any classification for bad fruits. This, however, was not the case. The postmodern soil could not escape producing bad fruits such as instilling people with a sense of burden in trying to discover their own meaning and causing a disconnect between people who can never agree on universal truths. The biggest bad fruit was mainly the sense of hopelessness that came with discovering that there was no metanarrative in the universe, and you were left wandering by yourself to discover meaning. Learning that this life is all you have, and you better find your own meaning in it is a dead-end for disaster because humans were never meant to take on such a lofty task.

This bad fruit caused the human tree to begin to uproot and plant itself into the soil of polarization. Fed up with trying to find its own meaning, humanity latched onto institutions and cults that defined their meaning for them. Although this soil hasn't played out to completion yet, I am confident it will because so far, it has followed the pattern of being contaminated with bad fruit. An ineffective way of dealing with the problem of evil and the quickness to judge are just a few.

So, what is the problem with the human tree? How could something as pure as religion turn into something as terrible as the crusades? How could something as beneficial to shaping society such as the enlightenment, create the bloodshed of the French Revolution? How could something that advanced society forward such as the industrial revolution, also send society flying backward in the World Wars? How could the simple motives of love and peace turn into drug abuse and hypocrisy? How could the prosperity of America turn into corruption and abuse of power seen in the funding of dictators? How could tolerance and better emphasis on emotions lead to the horrific destruction of truth and evil altogether? How could the natural desire for meaning and purpose cause the harsh judgment and toxic atmosphere we experience today? Was the soil to blame? Has humanity for all of its history, just been a failed gardening experiment, failing to choose the right soil to plant itself in over and over again? I do not think this is the case. Time and time again the human tree has replanted and replanted to get rid of the bad fruit with no success. The real issue was not, however, where they were planting. It was not the societal pressure to do evil. It was not the systematic institutions of evil in the world. The problem was not the soil. The human tree was desperately sick at the roots.

We now come to the same conclusion that the Bible has been preaching for over 2000 years. Humanity is not "naturally good" or comprised of "basically good people", we are sinful and naturally inclined for evil. In Jeremiah 17:9 we see that "The heart is deceitful above all things and beyond cure. Who can understand it?". This has been the condition of humanity ever since the original sin in the

Garden of Eden. Even as early as Genesis, we see God revealing the nature of the human heart. "Never again will I curse the ground because of humans, even though every inclination of the human heart is evil from childhood. And never again will I destroy all living creatures, as I have done." (Genesis 8:21). In the New Testament, again and again, our condition is affirmed. In Ephesians: "among whom we all once lived in the passions of our flesh, carrying out the desires of the body and the mind, and were by nature children of wrath, like the rest of mankind." (Ephesians 2:3). In Romans, Paul states that "None is righteous, no, not one; no one understands; no one seeks for God…no one does good, not even one" (Romans 3:10-11). One of the most powerful examples of the human condition is found in Psalm 51. For some context, David, the author of this Psalm, has just committed adultery and murdered the husband to cover it up. He has also just lied to the prophet Nathan. His confession to God, however, doesn't seem to address any of these issues. Instead, he confesses the heart of the issue behind all of the "bad fruits" produced in his life. He says "Behold, I was brought forth in iniquity, and in sin did my mother conceive me" (Psalm 51:5). David doesn't mention his adultery, murder, or lying at all in the confession, but mentions his corrupt nature that is bent towards sin. Following his example, we can start to get a glimpse of what it is like to really address the root problem rather than just getting rid of the bad fruits.

It is not just in the Bible that we find this idea that lies at the roots of human evil and suffering. Aleksandr Solzhenitsyn, a survivor of the horrific Soviet gulags in the 20th century, and a well renowned Russian author, had much to say about the human condition after his own experiences. After escaping the camps, he wrote *Gulag Archipelago* [1], a description of the Soviet work camps and the awful things that go on there. As he gets to the end of the novel, he gives valuable insight into the human heart:

"If only there were evil people somewhere insidiously committing evil deeds, and it were necessary only to separate them from the rest of us and destroy them. But the line dividing good and evil cuts through the heart of every human being. And who is willing to destroy a piece of his own heart?"

After spending a good amount of time in the very institution that was responsible for the deaths of 1.5-1.7 million individuals, he had every reason to conclude that evil was a systemic thing and that these people that were dying weren't evil, just victims of the corrupt and evil system that was the Soviet Union. This was not the conclusion that he came to, however, and it speaks volumes to the vast intellect that he possessed. He was able to diagnose the problem behind the problem and realize that behind the Gulag, behind the evil Soviet Union, were hearts that were bent towards evil. In his commencement address to Harvard in 1978, Solzhenitsyn gives the students the following advice regarding humanism and the heart:

"If humanism were right in declaring that man is born to be happy, he would not be born to die. Since his body is doomed to die, his task on earth evidently must be of a more spiritual nature. It cannot unrestrained enjoyment of everyday life. It cannot be the search for the best ways to obtain material goods and then cheerfully get the most out of them. It has to be the fulfillment of a permanent, earnest duty so that one's life journey may become an experience of moral growth, so that one may leave life a better human being than one started it. It is imperative to review the table of widespread human values. Its present incorrectness is astounding. It is not possible that assessment of the President's performance be reduced to the question of how much money one makes or of unlimited availability of gasoline. Only voluntary, inspired self-restraint can raise man above the world stream of materialism. It would be retrogression to attach oneself today to the ossified formulas of the Enlightenment. Social dogmatism leaves us completely helpless in front of the trials of our times." [2]

Augustine and the Human Heart

One of the chief patrons of this particular part of a Biblical worldview was Saint Augustine of Hippo. Living in the 4th century AD, he was a prominent theologian and philosopher of his time. During his life, he wrote *Confessions* [3], an honest novel of confession of sins and thought patterns he had held in his life. In this novel, we see a powerful image of what it looks like to correctly identify the problem of the roots inside of the human heart.

In Book 2, he retells a story from his childhood about stealing a pear from somebody else's tree. He goes into great analysis trying to discover the reason that he stole the pear. He first looks at systemic issues such as poverty and necessity, and comes to the conclusion that he didn't steal the pear because he was hungry, or even because he was poor and needed the pear. He stole it just for the sake of stealing it. After reflecting on this story, Augustine goes on to reveal something about the human heart that cuts to the very core of the problem and is still a sentiment felt by nearly everyone today. He says: "I loved self-destruction, I loved my fall, not the object for which I had fallen, but my fall itself. My depraved soul leaped down from your firmament of ruin". It is precisely this sentiment that keeps us in so many sinful patterns today: our hearts love the taste of sin and are bent towards doing evil. Later in the enlightenment, Rousseau would come to a conclusion that was different than Augustine's, but it led to widespread evil, corruption, and the bloodshed of the French Revolution. What was this conclusion? In his famous novel *The Social Contract*, he came to the conclusion that "People in their natural state are basically good. But this natural innocence however is corrupted by the evils of society". Coming to the opposite conclusion of Augustine, he misdiagnosed the human condition at the roots and therefore pushed for soil change, which was actualized in the French Revolution. This is why it is so important to get the human condition right. If you don't, then society will be caught in an endless loop of bad systems without really addressing the root problems behind the evils those systems cause.

Augustine fully grasped the corruption of his own heart, not just because he understood the human condition, but because he understood the relationship between God and man. He states that "Things get corrupted because they aren't the supreme good". This understanding of the supreme goodness and holiness of God can further help us understand our condition. It can sometimes be very hard to look at the world (at least not very far into the world) and conclude that people are naturally bent towards evil. If you live in an affluent country and a wealthy neighborhood where everyone is nice and gives to charity and helps feed the homeless and goes to church once and a while, it can seem like the natural man is bent towards good deeds. These sentiments, however, are blown out of the waters by thinking of those "good deeds" in comparison to a supremely good and perfect God who created the universe. This is exactly what Augustine does when he feels that these sentiments are getting a hold of him and even devotes an entire section of his own confessions to reflecting on God's character.

"Then I turned towards myself, and said to myself: "Who are you? I replied: 'A man.' I see in myself a body and a soul, one external, the other internal. Which of these should I have questioned about my God, for whom I had already searched through the physical order of things from earth to heaven, as far as I could send the rays of my eyes? As messengers? What is inward is superior. All physical evidence is reported to the mind which presides and judges of the responses of heaven and earth and all things in them, as they say, 'We are not God' and 'He made us'. The inner man knows this-I, I the mind through the sense-perception of my body. I asked the mass of the sun about my God, and it replied to me: 'It is not I, but he made me."

Augustine understood the weightiness of God and correctly understood the human condition in light of a comparison to the glory that even surpassed the sun. May we strive to gain such a deep understanding of our God that it brings us to our knees in confession like Augustine and like Paul. If you get your concept of God right, you will get the state of humanity right with it.

How did we flip this fundamental problem?

The deceitfulness and evil of the human heart are some of the most fundamental parts of being human in a fallen world. More than racial identity, nationality, economic class, job title, gender, or even personality, our status as sinners before an all-righteous God is our main identifier throughout the Bible. Humanity is sick at its roots and that is a Biblical truth. So how did we come to a place in time where this very statement would be seen as hate speech, or divisive? How can there be churches out there teaching that man is inherently good and must "unlock his inner potential", to quote Joel Osteen, the pastor of one of the largest churches in America. I think that the problem starts with a fundamental misunderstanding about God.

Without a Biblical view of God who is "holy, holy, holy" to quote Isaiah, and cannot dwell in the presence of sin, the doctrine of humanity falls apart. When you get God's sovereignty and holiness wrong by overemphasizing human free will and control, then you will slowly be replacing God's throne with a human ruler. This can be seen plainly with the secular movement, as religion was replaced with man in places such as the Soviet Union, and Nazi Germany. Hitler thought of himself as a god and viewed his own race as good people. This can be seen very widespread today, as we live in a majority secular culture. Many of the social justice advocates start off with the assumption that the human heart is basically good, so it baffles them when peaceful protests turn into riots, or good movements produce selfish individuals who are power-hungry. A skewed view of humanity as basically good also produces a culture of self-righteousness because, without a God, humans must fill the "righteousness gap".

Inside of the church, however, it is slightly harder to spot the dethroning of God. Many of the churches associated with the word of faith or prosperity movement look an awfully lot like normal Christianity from the outside. They have spectacular worship, read the same Bible we do and seem like good people on the outside. What many do though, is warp God so that he is all about us. God exists so that we can live happy lives and be blessed with great success and jobs. Many of these churches also teach the "little gods doctrine" that states that we are basically little gods waiting to reach our full potential. Can you see how this fundamental error in the nature of God and his motivation drives the entire ship off course? These churches are no different from the secular culture in misdiagnosing the human condition and replacing God's throne with a mere mortal.

To get humanity right, you must understand that the God of the Bible's primary motivation behind all that he does isn't that we can become blessed, although he does bless us. God's primary goal is to bring glory to his own name. God exists to maximize his own glory, and he does this not in our *independence*, but in our *dependence* on him. In one of his most famous sermons, Jonathan Edwards, a Great Awakening preacher in the 1700s, gave a message titled "God Glorified in Man's dependence" [4]. In this sermon, he dissects 1 Corinthians 1:29-31: "so that no one may boast before him. It is because of him that you are in Christ Jesus, who has become for us wisdom from God—that is, our righteousness, holiness, and redemption. Therefore, as it is written: "Let the one who boasts boast in the Lord.". Edwards proclaimed that "God's goal in redemption is that man should glory in God alone", and that "All good that humanity has is through Christ". At this time in American history (when America wasn't even its own country yet), independence and living on one's own were ideas of chief importance. That is the main reason that many came to America in the first place: to have the freedom of religion from England. Edward's sermon radically spoke to that audience and caused a revival in their view of God and their relationship to him. I think that this same message could cause a revival today if it were given across word of faith and prosperity churches. Self-righteous, anthropocentric, churchgoers desperately need to hear that God is mainly concerned with pursuing his own glory, and in doing so, he is maximally glorified in humanity's dependence.

The word "repent" as it is sometimes used in the New Testament comes from the Greek word Metanoia, which means "to rethink your thinking". In the Church, we need to rethink our thinking constantly and correct false concepts of God that lead to dangerous conclusions about the human race. Likewise, the Church should be an influencer in the world and reshape the secular view of humanity as "basically good", in order to be able to accurately fight injustice and diagnose complex problems in our current age.

Treating the Roots, Not Just the Fruits

One of the major applications of the human condition for today's soil is that it shifts the way that we approach social justice and fighting injustice in our world. Knowing that the problem is in the roots of the human tree gives us a whole new method of addressing corrupt systems that is more in line with how Jesus addressed and thought about the problems of his day.

Around the time that Jesus started his ministry, nearly 1/3rd of the Roman world was enslaved. Given that rough estimations of the population of the Roman empire at this time come out to about 56.8 million people, that is nearly 19 million people in slavery. Sure, slavery was a little different and more humane back then, but still, these people didn't have freedom and were attached to their masters. If we were looking at a systemic approach, this widespread slavery was a corrupt system that needed reform and removal, and what better man to do it than the son of God himself, Jesus. If we look at Jesus's ministry, however, he does not address this corrupt system at all. In fact, he hardly addresses any of the corrupt systems of the Roman empire that the Jews thought he would. They were expecting a warrior king who would free them from the oppression of the Romans, who had complete jurisdiction over them, not someone who said, "give unto Caesar what is Caesar's" (Matthew 22:21). Even Palm Sunday and the yelling of "Hosanna" was a battle cry in hopes that Jesus would overthrow the corrupt systems of the day.

This is not why Jesus came. He says it himself in Luke 19:10, "The Son of Man came to seek and save the lost". This of course came as a bamboozlement to the Jewish people as they saw the problems of their day, not with people, but with the corrupt systems. When Jesus didn't do anything about the systems, they were confused and started to lose faith and hope in him, and eventually hung him on a cross. Jesus came to treat the root of the problem, not just the fruits. He came to save sinners, not try and redeem broken systems. He knew what the real problem was behind the evils of the world. He knew that it was the corrupt human heart, not just the corrupt human systems in place.

Treating the fruits without treating the roots is, for the most part, ineffective. Bad fruits, as hopefully, you have seen throughout the novel, keep popping up out of the human tree despite what soil it is planted in. Once one bad fruit is treated, two more will pop up in its place and the root issue will go unchecked. It is as though you are trying to treat a bullet wound with a hello kitty band-aid. It isn't going to help at all and could even cause more harm than good because left unchecked, the human heart can go rampant with pride.

So how does all of this inform how we do our social justice today? I think that we can have two main takeaways from the life of Jesus, which should inform how we deal with injustice in the world.

The Gospel is the First Thing

C.S. Lewis once famously said, "Put first things first and second things are thrown in. Put second things first and you lose both first and second things.". I think that this idea should shape the way that we look at social justice in our world. Social justice is not a "first thing". It will not save you; it will not transform you. The Gospel, that Jesus came down to earth to save sinners like you and me, should be the first thing. Any form of social justice that loses sight of this first thing, won't really be addressing the root problem of the human heart. As we will see in the next chapter, only the Gospel and God have the ability to change the human heart. Behind every injustice, we should see the hearts that are bent towards evil and in desperate need of reconciliation and the transformation that comes with the Holy Spirit. Jesus came to seek and save the lost and we should do the same. We should be ministers of social justice not for social justice's sake, but for the sake of the Gospel. Everything we

do should advance this good news throughout the nations.
We should say with Paul, "I do all this for the sake of the
gospel, that I may share in its blessings." [5].

The Gospel should propel us into social justice. This
is an example of the second things being "thrown in" when
we put the first things first. If we are striving towards a
Gospel-centered living like Jesus, then it will follow that
we will heal the sick and help the widow and the orphan
like he did. If you are seeking first the "gospel" but it
doesn't result in you wanting to do something about the
injustices in the world, then I'd highly urge you to
reconsider whether the gospel you are following is, in fact,
the Christian one, or just simply the "American Gospel"
that is mainly concerned with health and wealth. If we keep
the Gospel of Jesus Christ as utmost importance, "that
Christ died for our sins in accordance with the Scriptures,
that he was buried, that he was raised on the third day in
accordance with the Scriptures", then social justice will
follow in a way that is glorifying to God.

So much of what is currently called social justice identifies the problems of humanity, like Rousseau: "out there". It is the corrupt systems, or the evil institutions in place that cause humans to act unjustly and despicably. Social justice therefore in this view, is mainly concerned with defeating systems. I hope that you've been able to see through the countless number of systems that have been defeated in this book, that this does not bring about the end of evil.

So much of our current efforts towards social justice, however, have not learned from history that treating the fruit does not work. For a modern example, let's take a look into the way that racism is being treated in our modern climate. Many are quick to call people out for making comments that are racist, or even calling people racists themselves because they support a certain president or group of people. If you don't protest or post something on your social media… "you are racist". If you do post something, but it is interpreted in a wrong way… "you are racist". These surface level problems are fruit issues. All we see in the media is attempts to treat the fruits by either cancelling certain individuals or calling for surface level reforms such as implicit bias training. This is what we should expect when we are looking at the problem, not as a root issue, but a fruit issue. When we identify the fruit of "systemic racism" it would make sense that the system naturally produces evil people that are racist because of their heritage or the deep, deep roots in American history. This way of thinking automatically groups people into categories. You are either an oppressor or oppressed according to the system that is in place and the problem is with the oppressors. They need to do something to fix the rigged system of racism so that the playing field is even. This, rather than cause racial unity, has caused much division between Church members, between neighbors, and between political parties. People are quite tired of being roped onto the "bad guy" team of history.

The problem isn't out there. The truth is not some simple thing that you can categorize as either this or that. The world is complex, and a complex world must understand that the problem is in here. Inside every human heart, there is an inclination for racism, for pride, for superiority, for destruction, for slander, and for evil. An honest and effective effort to rid the world of evil should begin with your own heart.

Now, you would be foolish to come away from this chapter thinking that you should not do anything to rid the evil systems of the world, or that so-called systems don't exist. Yes, there are in fact many evil systems in the world such as dictatorship regimes in North Korea, oppression of women in the middle east, and the caste systems of India to name a few. To not speak out and take action against these systems would be the wrong thing to do. The point I am trying to make in this chapter is that you shouldn't stop with the destruction of the system. You should go further than the system and realize that the corrupt human heart is behind it all and the only thing that can change that is the Gospel of Jesus Christ.

The *Times of London* [6] at one point early in the 1900s posed this question to several prominent authors: "What's wrong with the world today?". Many authors responded with long essays on corrupt systems that were in place, evil leaders that led citizens astray, natural consequences to a naturally selected world, and everything in between. But one response to the prompt stands out. G.K. Chesterton, a Christian writer and theologian responded to the Times with this simple response. When asked what is wrong with the world, he responded:

"Dear Sir,

I am.

Yours, G.K. Chesterton".

10

HEALING THE ROOTS

How then, do we go about healing the roots of the human tree's problem? If I were a Buddhist, I'd tell you to follow the eightfold path towards enlightenment. If I were a Mormon, I would tell you to obey the Word of Wisdom, get baptized in the temple, become sealed, and perform temple ordinances. If I were a Word of Faith Prosperity teacher, I would give you 10 tips on how to unlock your inner potential. If I were a Hindu, I would tell you that you are stuck where you are in the caste system and you can hope for a better life in the next reincarnation. If I were a Muslim, I would tell you to keep the five pillars and trust Allah's mercy. If I were a nihilist, I would tell you that healing the roots is impossible and you should just accept it.

If I were a postmodernist, I would tell you to "do what you feel is right" and that there is no right or wrong way to heal the root of the problem, it is all subjective. If I were a humanist, I would deny that the problem existed altogether. But I am not any of these things, I am a Christian, and the Christian Gospel offers something radically different than every other worldview in dealing with the problem of the human heart—as you will come to see (or have already seen) in your own life.

So what does the Christian Gospel, the good news of Jesus Christ, offer as a solution? The presentation of the Gospel in Paul's letter to the Romans sheds some light on the situation. It begins with nearly 3 whole chapters explaining the unrighteousness of man in great detail. This, of course, isn't the solution, it is the problem. So why does Paul use so much ink to talk about our human state? He seems to value the reader recognizing their position before a righteous God. Dwelling on your own unrighteousness and sin is a very healthy practice, as it does wonders to put in perspective the holiness and righteousness of God in light of the divide between us and him.

But if you were to remain your whole life dwelling on the unrighteousness of man, you would be foolish and acting in a manner that is largely un-Christlike. For Romans doesn't end after 3 chapters of reflection on humanity's unrighteousness. Directly following Romans 3:23, "For all have sinned and fall short of the glory of God", comes the hope of Romans 3:24, "[You] are justified by his grace as a gift through the redemption that is in Christ Jesus.". If Romans ended at 3:23, then the good news of the gospel would hardly be good news at all. But it doesn't end there. Although we are called unrighteous, Christ was righteous for us and through his death, he justified us, a forensic term meaning Christ imputes his righteousness on us, by his grace alone. Through this act of grace, Christ makes us righteous before God and saves us from our state of unrighteousness. According to scripture alone, the way that the heart condition is truly changed and the way we are saved is by grace alone through faith alone in Christ alone so that God and God alone get all the glory. This is the good news that separates Christianity from every other major world religion. We are not the transformers of our own heart; it is God that saves us.

The question now is how do we go about this heart transformation? How do we accept the free gift of grace that is presented to us if we ourselves are naturally inclined to do evil, not good, and in our hearts "there is no fear of God" (Romans 3:18)? I don't believe that we can on our own will. We are utterly corrupted by the sin in our lives and in Ephesians 2:1-3 we see that we are in a condition of complete spiritual death.

"As for you, you were dead in your transgressions and sins, in which you used to live when you followed the ways of this world and of the ruler of the kingdom of the air, the spirit who is now at work in those who are disobedient. All of us also lived among them at one time, gratifying the cravings of our flesh and following its desires and thoughts. Like the rest, we were by nature deserving of wrath"

Even in the Old Testament, God's work on transforming hearts can be seen. In Deuteronomy 30 we find that the heart is uncircumcised, a symbol of being cut off from God's covenant. In Ezekiel 36, we find that our hearts are like that of stone, unable to give life to our bodies. In Jeremiah 31, we find that our hearts have forgotten the law, God's covenant with his people.

In all of these instances, it is clear that the human heart is unable to help itself. It is a hardened, uncircumcised, law-forgetting, spiritually dead entity unable to accept the free gift of grace that is necessary to redeem the heart. So how does it happen? How is the heart truly redeemed? Well, if you take the time to read these chapters and verses in their entirety, you will find that they don't just end with a hopeless humanity and a disgusting-looking heart either. In Deuteronomy 30:6, we find that : "The Lord your God will circumcise your hearts and the hearts of your descendants, so that you may love him with all your heart and with all your soul, and live." In Ezekiel 35:26, God says "I will give you a new heart and put a new spirit in you; I will remove from you your heart of stone and give you a heart of flesh." In Jeremiah 31:33 God says, "I will put my law in their minds and write it on their hearts. I will be their God, and they will be my people." And the terrible news that was our condition in Ephesians 2:1-3 is interrupted in Ephesians 2:4-5, "But because of his great love for us, God, who is rich in mercy, made us alive with Christ even when we were dead in transgressions—it is by grace you have been saved."

We can now see who the real hero in the salvation story is. It is not us, who made the heroic and daring choice to choose God, it was he who made the choice to save us and make our hearts beat with life for him. If this chapter were to be titled "10 ways to heal your heart today" that it would be nothing but wishful thinking. We do not have the power to change our own hearts, only God can do that, because he crafted each and every one of us and fully knows the condition we are all in. We can be radically transformed from death to life not from our own power, but by the grace of God.

This radical transformation can be best seen in the life of Saul, a first-century persecutor of Christians. Saul was a firm opponent to Jesus and the entire Christian movement; he executed Christians and was even seen approving of the apostle Stephen's stoning. But Saul's deceitful and murderous heart was suddenly interrupted by the grace of God. When the resurrected Jesus appeared to Saul on the road to Damascus, his entire heart changed and he became a minister of the gospel, writing a large portion of the New Testament under his transformed name, Paul. If we look more closely into the story, we see that it is clear that Saul did not choose God. Jesus did not appear to Saul on the road and then give him a few hours to think about whether he really wanted to accept Jesus given all of the historical arguments, or logical reasoning it took to get there. Saul was transformed and could not reject the transformation that had occurred in his life. Saul could not have merely seen the resurrected Jesus and then went on killing all of his followers.

A more modern example of how God is still radically transforming hearts is seen in the transformation of John Newton. You may not be fully acquainted with Newton, but he is most well-known for his hymn "Amazing Grace." John Newton was born in 1725 England, where the Trans-Atlantic Slave Trade had just begun to ramp up, now that the Americas were colonized. Newton was one of the slave traders and worked on a ship that transported slaves from Africa to England and the Americas. On one of those voyages, there was a great storm that lasted several days, leaving the sailors with little hope of survival. During this storm, God tugged on Newton's heart in the time or distress and he gave his life to Christ. Newton recognized during this storm that he wasn't in total control of his circumstances and life, and that he was in desperate need of a savior. After their boat miraculously docked in Ireland, Newton was a transformed man. Through Christ slowly changing his vision to see the world and people as God does, Newton had gone from a slave trader to a staunch abolitionist and would eventually go on with William Wilberforce to completely abolish slavery in England. In the words of his famous song, John Newton powerfully encapsulates the feeling of transformation. "Amazing Grace, how sweet the sound That saved a wretch like me. I once was lost, but now am found. Was blind but now I see."

So, after their heart transformations, were Paul and Newton completely holy and perfect? By no means! Anyone can locate an example of someone who you know who has converted to Christianity that is still living in sin and is nowhere near perfect. We now find ourselves in a Biblical tension. On the one hand, our hearts are transformed from their old ways, but on the other, they are still bent towards the old ways and we still aren't perfect.

Even Paul admits in Romans 7:15 that, "I do not understand what I do. For what I want to do I do not do, but what I hate I do." How is it that heart transformation brings about such an imperfect result? The key to understanding this is to understand the difference between justification and sanctification.

While God transforms our hearts and makes us positionally righteous before himself, we can clearly see that we are not yet *practically* righteous in everyday life. We still cheat, steal, lie, slander, and do all sorts of unrighteous things in our day to day life even after our hearts are transformed by God. The truth of the Christian life affirms that salvation and heart transformation is not a one and done deal. They are ongoing processes that must be dealt with daily. Jesus says to us that "If anyone desires to come after me, let him deny himself, and take up his cross daily, and follow me.'" (Luke 9:23). In Philippians, we see the Christian journey portrayed as something that doesn't simply end with conversion and in fact continues until Christ's return, "For I am confident of this very thing, that He who began a good work in you will perfect it until the day of Christ Jesus." (1:6). It goes on to explain our role in this process, "Brothers, join in imitating me and keep your eyes on those who walk according to the example you have in us" (3:17). So, while justification is becoming positionally righteous, sanctification-is the process in which the believer strives towards becoming *practically* what he already is positionally.

To give an example of this, let's take the *position* of the president. One can be positionally a president without practically doing any of the things a president does. If a president goes out into the world and eats at McDonald's, spends all of his time vacationing in Hawaii, and never spends any of his time signing bills or governing his country, then he isn't practically being a president. In fact, it would make you question whether his presidency was actually real at all. This is the same as the believer. A true believer should be striving to live a righteous life and to reflect the life of Jesus in their own lives to his glory.

A Quick Overview of Complete Heart Transformation [1]

When do you know that your heart is completely transformed? When you are exactly like Jesus. This will, unfortunately, never happen in this life, and we will only fully achieve our positional righteousness in the process of glorification, our state of perfected righteousness. In this final stage of salvation —which is guaranteed by God's power and by Scripture— we will receive resurrection bodies to fully take on perfected righteousness. But we are not there yet and are currently living in a period of sanctification, so let's fix our eyes on the specifics of what complete heart transformation looks like in the day to day life in order to strive towards it with full responsibility.

A completely transformed heart will perfectly reflect Jesus in his capacity to reason Biblically, logically, and with deep awareness of the worldviews around him. Jesus knew the Bible so well that it was his go-to response whenever someone asked him a question or tried to critique him. One of his most common responses recorded in the Gospels is "is it not written" followed by a quote from Old Testament scripture. If we are to truly mirror Jesus, we must respond to hard problems and situations not with secular ideas, but with Biblical ideas and principles. Jesus also represented a deep level of logical thinking which he used to outwit the Sadducees in Matthew 22:23-27. This means that we shouldn't just go out into the complex world full of complex problems without bringing our brains. You do not need to sacrifice logic in the face of peer pressure or the fear of what another group may think of you. To truly reflect the mind of Christ, logic is essential. This statement means that your education matters to God. Each time you learn Philosophy, Biology, Chemistry, Psychology, Literature, or History in a way that is honoring to God, you are becoming more Christlike in that you are fulfilling the great commandment to love the Lord your God with all your heart, soul, *mind*, and strength.

A completely transformed heart will also mirror the emotional life of Jesus and respond to all situations with valid emotions. In our world today, feelings are seen as valid if they are felt, especially if they are feelings felt by a group that our society labels as "oppressed." While this works sometimes, this is not how feelings are meant to work and it is certainly not how Jesus viewed feelings. In his work, *The Abolition of Man* [2], C.S. Lewis tackles this problem through a story about a children's book that is threatening to destroy the world. This book titled *The Green Book* is an entire children's book about how feelings are arbitrary. It has made an attempt to separate feelings from facts and therefore they become unfalsifiable because only facts are thought about as being proven true or false. This is not how feelings were expressed by Jesus, as they cannot be separated from facts. Walking through the corrupt temple courtyards in John 2:13-16, Jesus would have been unjust if he had simply ignored all of the corruption that was going on. If he had just walked by, I think we could all agree that he did not express a valid feeling in response to the injustice. The story of Jesus at the temple shows us that it is important to respond to injustice around us. It would be an invalid feeling to be passive towards it all. If we are to be mirroring Jesus with a completely transformed heart, we need to take action and feel disgusted towards the injustices of the world. Christians have been doing this for centuries as they led the abolition movements, helped widows and unwanted orphans in the human dumps of ancient Rome, and many other amazing things that have been mentioned previously in this book.

A completely transformed heart will follow Jesus in his view of power as well. In order to understand this concept of power, we must first take a look at what the common perspective towards power is today. Power is commonly associated with presidents and high-up business moguls. It is often seen as a negative thing, something that oppresses those without power and something that we need to get rid of. This view of power is very much in line with philosopher Fredrich Nietzsche, who in his work *Will to Power* [3] describes power as a 0-sum game. You must take power from others to have it yourself, and in order for you to gain more power, somebody else must decrease in power. Even Jesus's disciples dealt with this kind of power during the Last Supper when they argued about who was the greatest disciple. Jesus quickly dismissed these power-hungry disciples by completely flipping their concept of power by saying "the one who is greatest among you must become like the youngest, and the one who leads like the one who serves" (Luke 22:26). Power in Jesus's view is not only something that elevates yourself but also elevates others. Real power, according to Jesus, elevates others rather than putting them down. We see this display of power when Jesus washed the disciple's feet. In this act of servanthood, we see that servanthood is the very purpose of a power that elevates others. Throughout the entire life of Jesus, this view of power as servanthood is proclaimed and it is summed up in Philippians 2. "Think this in yourselves which was also in Christ Jesus, who, existing in the form of God, did not consider being equal with God something to be grasped, but emptied himself by taking the form of a slave, by becoming in the likeness of people. And being found in appearance like a man, he humbled himself by becoming obedient to the point of death, that is, death on a cross. Therefore, also God exalted him and graciously granted him the name above every name." (Philippians 2:5-9). Jesus had every right to claim power over others, but used that power to serve and give his life as a sacrifice. So, what does this look like in our world today? We should be seeking a kind of power that doesn't destroy others on the way to the top. We should consider others before ourselves and see our power as an opportunity to serve those around us.

A completely transformed heart will love like Jesus, as well as express every fruit of the Spirit. In John 17, we get a beautiful prayer given by Jesus that shows us how to live in love as he did. In verse 24, we see that the Father loved the Son before the foundation of the world. This demonstrates that love is the most ancient thing in existence: before the world existed, there was love existing between the members of the Trinity. We were created out of love, meaning that we are hardwired for love expressed in community. Love in a Biblical sense is very much an action and not just a feeling as we use the word today. To love, there must be another person involved. In fact, the first malediction in the entire Bible is "It is not good for man to be alone," from Genesis 2:18. To mirror the love of Jesus, we must seek out community, not push it away. In John 17:23, we see another insight into loving like Jesus: it acknowledges a fundamental truth that God loves us like he loves Jesus. Let that sink in for a moment. This is the most fundamentally true thing about yourself: you are loved by God with the same weightiness and divine glory that he loves Jesus with. This foundation is more unshakable than any worldly identity and should be the foundation of our love for others. "We love because he first loved us," as 1 John 4:19 puts it. In John 17:22, we see that Jesus also prays for unity among believers. A premise to this petition for unity is the knowledge that God actually has the ability to create unity and love where it is lacking. Mirroring the love of Jesus involves relying on the supernatural love of God, not just human effort, to create unity in this divisive world.

Basically, what I am getting at in this section is that a completely transformed heart will mirror Jesus in every aspect of his life. It will love God with all heart, soul, mind, and strength. It will recognize its own corruption and give God all the glory for its transformation. In our world today, heart change is a rarity. Real heart change, as seen by our culture, is next to impossible. A popular sentiment that I have seen floating around is "People don't change, their masks just fall off." If this is our culture's view of the changing heart, then they haven't seen the extent of heart change that can come with believing in Jesus as Lord and Savior. People have gone from death to life, from rejected to adopted, from slave to free in Jesus. From a Christian worldview, heart change is possible; in fact, it is expected of those who confess belief in Jesus. It isn't just masks falling off, it is scales falling off of a hardened heart as God is working to restore it to himself.

A Case Study in Self-Help

The most prominent way that so many Americans, even those professing to be Christian, try and deal with the heart problem is through self-help programs. In fact, almost every world religion besides Christianity is, at its core, a self-help program. In these programs, humans are basically good people and all they really need Jesus for is to help them go from good to great. All they need the Bible for is to make them feel blessed and entitled. All they need the church for is to reinforce their thinking and make them feel good inside. They will do all of these religious practices to gain blessings, or to achieve eternal happiness for themselves. With the popularity of this thought pattern, I thought it would be appropriate to study whether the self-help program actually changes the heart. To do this, we must look at what is arguably the longest-running self-help program in the history of the world and see the results. We must look at the story of Israel.

The story of Israel as a large nation began with enslavement in Egypt. After escaping slavery with the help of Moses and ultimately God, they wandered in the desert for 40 years. In their time of wandering, they were given the ultimate instruction manual for righteousness: The Ten Commandments. Just like modern self-help books, it had a set of rules to follow and it had a reward for keeping those rules. Although the Ten Commandments were never meant to be a path to salvation, the Israelites tried hard to keep the law. In the end, however, they broke it. Heck, they pretty much broke the law the second it was given to them by worshiping a golden calf as an idol rather than God (Exodus 32).

After Israel had been established in the Promised Land, they began to offer sacrifices to God performed by priests. This was the traditional way to cleanse yourself from sin. Even something as pure as sacrifice though was corrupted by the priests, who themselves became malevolent.

Israel then entered into a period of the judges, people who God appointed to rule and correct the wrongs of the people. After vicious cycles of disobedience and not doing what God had commanded, the era of the judges eventually ended with everyone doing what was right in their own eyes (Judges 21:25).

Then Israel begged for a ruler and was begrudgingly given the chance to pick a king for themselves by God. They chose their tallest, most handsome guy to save them from the surrounding kingdoms. This prized figure, however, became selfish and strayed from God.

The people were then given prophets to inform the kings of God and tell them what to do. This sounds great at first, but then the people kill the prophets.

What is the result? Israel is eventually broken up and thrust into exile. Losing their land, their people, and their blessing that was promised as part of the covenant from God to Abraham. The plan of self-help, trying to earn their own salvation, purify themselves, and choose their own rulers, ended in utter disaster.

What God was doing with the Israelites was to show that self-help strategies cannot save. Through the entire Old Testament, it is clear that we need a better law-keeper than ourselves if we are going to be righteous in God's eyes. We need a better sacrifice and a better priest that will truly take away our sins. We need a better judge who will be fair and just and keep people from confusion. We need a better king that isn't corrupted with selfishness. We need a better prophet that truly speaks for God. We need Jesus.

All self-help strategies fail to help the actual problem of the heart precisely because of who is doing the helping: yourself. The self was never meant to fight the problem of sin and death that only Jesus through his death and resurrection fought for us. In fact, how could you possibly beat the problem of sin if you yourself are by nature a sinner? It would be like a drunkard trying to help another drunkard get sober while drinking alcohol. It just won't work.

The Greatest Tree Story in Existence

We now return to the tree at the beginning of human history to find the root of the problem. In the Garden of Eden, Adam and Eve were presented with the tree of the knowledge of good and evil. This was the one tree that God had told them not to eat from because humanity was never meant to define good and evil apart from God. Of course, as the story goes, they did eat from the tree after being tempted by the serpent. This initial fall of man was caused by worshiping the creation over the Creator, which by the standards of the Bible, is idolatry. This fall caused the separation in the perfect relationship between God and man and made it impossible for us to be in his presence. You can see this in the fact that they hid in a tree from God right after they had eaten the fruit.

This separation from God happened by a tree, but the story of human history doesn't end there. Although humanity fell by a tree and hid behind a tree after sinning, humanity was also redeemed by a tree. The tree that Jesus died on to restore our relationship to God, if we believe in him, is the ultimate "tree story" in all of history. So take this book as a simple mirror. This story isn't the greatest tree story and never claims to be so. The story of the human tree isn't the greatest tree story because humanity isn't the center of history. The greatest tree story to exist is also the most tragic. The greatest tree story is one that actually happened in real space and time. It is the story of Jesus that has implications for every single one of us. The human tree is not stuck in an endless cycle of trying to help itself address its soil problems. The story of Jesus entered into our human story to usher in the "age to come" in which all of the current rules of the world don't apply. Redemption is possible, heart change is possible, and it is being done daily by the work of Christ alone. We can celebrate the fact that the human tree is not the end-all, be-all story of history. The human tree does not even play the main role in the greatest tree story. We are part of the problem in the story. We are desperately sick at our roots. The moment we begin to realize this and shift our gaze upon the glory of God, real heart change begins. We are brought into the greatest redemption story of all time. May God receive all of the glory for the planting, sustaining, transformation, and fruit of the human tree.

The End.

NOTES AND WORKS CITED

Chapter 1: The Tree of Life

1. Wohlleben, Peter. *The Hidden Life of Trees*. Vancouver: Greystone Books, 2018.

2. Athanasius, Penelope Lawson, and C. S. Lewis. *On the Incarnation*. Place of publication not identified: publisher not identified, 2013.

3. For further reading on the subject, see Rosenberg, Stanley P., Michael Burdett, Michael Lloyd, and Benno van den Toren. *Finding Ourselves after Darwin Conversations on the Image of God, Original Sin, and the Problem of Evil*. Grand Rapids: Baker Academic, 2018.

Chapter 2: The Soil of Religion

1. Stark, Rodney. *The Rise of Christianity: How the Obscure, Marginal Jesus Movement Became the*

Dominant Religious Force in the Western World in a Few Centuries. San Francisco: Harper Collins Publishers, 1997.

2. There are very fringe groups of people that think things such as increased science and education aren't good things, and most are in the Church ironically. While they might be a counterpoint to this criterion for good fruit, I am trying to make the point that they *should* see these as good fruits because they are. Good and bad are always more complex than what I have prescribed in this book. I simplify it to make a point because this book isn't mainly about good and evil.

3. https://handbook.fas.harvard.edu/book/history

4. Sims, Walter Hines. *Baptist Hymnal*. Convention Press, n.d.

5. Ben-David, Joseph. *Scientific Growth: a Sociological View*, 1964.

6. Harrison, Peter. *The Territories of Science and Religion*. Chicago: The University of Chicago Press, 2017.

7. Condivi, Ascanio, and Charles Robertson. *The Life of Michelangelo*. London: Athene, 2013.

8. Hill, Rosalind Mary Theodosia. *Gesta Francorum Et Aliorum Hierosolimitanorum - The Deeds of the Franks and the Other Pilgrims to Jerusalem*. New-York: T. Nelson, 1962.

9. A quick note on the Crusades: In actuality, the Christians were fairly justified in fighting the Islamic forces because they had attacked first and threatened the extinction of their people. But I do think that the crusaders went too far in their assault and caused a lot of gratuitous violence that was not necessary for their purpose.

10. Luther, Martin. *95 Theses*. Orem, UT: Western Standard Publishing Company, 2013.

11. "Native American Indian Culture: Rituals, Dances and Ceremonies." The People's Paths Resource, April 23, 2018. http://www.yvwiiusdinvnohii.net/native-american-indian-culture-rituals-dances-and-ceremonies/.

12. Columbus, Christopher. "The Gilder Lehrman
Institute of American History." Columbus reports
on his first voyage, 1493 | Gilder Lehrman Institute
of American History. Accessed June 16, 2020.
www.gilderlehrman.org/content/columbus-reports-
his-first-voyage-1493.

Chapter 3: The Soil of Secularism

1. Descartes, Rene. *Meditations on First Philosophy*.
Place of publication not identified: Simon &
Brown, 2018.

2. Kant, Immanuel. *Foundations of the Metaphysics
of Morals, and What Is Enlightenment?*
Indianapolis: Bobbs-Merrill, 1959.

3. Locke, John, Ernest Barker, David Hume, and
Jean-Jacques Rousseau. *Social Contract: Essays*.
Place of publication not identified: publisher not
identified, 2010.

4. Tocqueville, Alexis de, and John Bonner. *The Old
Regime and the French Revolution*. Mineola, NY:
Dover Publications, 2010.

5. Bon, Gustave Le. *Psychology of Revolution*. Place of publication not identified: Alpha Editions, 2018.

6. Burke, Edmund. *Reflections on the Revolution in France*. Overland Park, KS: Digireads, 2018.

Chapter 4: The Soil of Technology and Innovation

1. Wing, Charles. *Evils of the Factory System: Demonstrated by Parliamentary Evidence*. London: Cass, 1967.

2. "Child Labor in the Industrial Revolution." History Crunch - History Articles, Summaries, Biographies, Resources and More. Accessed June 17, 2020. https://www.historycrunch.com/child-labor-in-the-industrial-revolution.html.

3. Poolos, Jamie. *The Atomic Bombings of Hiroshima and Nagasaki*. New York: Chelsea House, 2008.

4. Remarque, Erich Maria, and Denver Lindley. *Flotsam: a Novel*. New York: Random House Trade Paperbacks, 2013.

Chapter 5: The Soil of Love and Peace

1. Rothman, Lily. "The Hippies, Philosophy of a Subculture." *Time*, July 7, 1967.

2. King, Martin Luther. "Beyond Vietnam." Speech, April 4, 1967.

3. Stevens, Jay. *Storming Heaven: LSD and the American Dream*. New York: Grove Press, 1998.

4. Chill, Gene, and John Duff. *The Truth about Drugs: the Body, Mind, and You*. Los Angeles, CA: Bridge Publications, 1981.

Chapter 6: The Soil of Economics

1. Smith, Adam. *The Wealth of Nations*. Lexington, KY: Seven Treasures Publications, 2009.

2. Marx, Karl, and Friedrich Engels. *The Communist Manifesto*. Singapore: Origami Books, 2020.

3. Galbraith, Kenneth. *The Affluent Society*. Penguin, 1991.

4. I am not saying that Capitalism is bad. If you look at the alternatives throughout history, they are

much worse. I am simply pointing out that any good thing can become corrupted and this was the case with capitalism and the thirst for power in the 20th century.

Chapter 7: The Soil of Postmodernism

1. I owe this marvelous map analogy to my wonderful philosophy professor Gregg TenElshof of Biola University.

2. Camus, Albert. *The Myth of Sysyphus, and Other Essays*. New York: Vintage Books, 1955.

3. Pelt, Doug Van. *Rock Stars on God*. Lake Mary, FL: Relevant Books, 2004.

4. "Stressed Nation: 74% of UK 'Overwhelmed or Unable to Cope' at Some Point in the Past Year." Mental Health Foundation, January 16, 2020. https://www.mentalhealth.org.uk/news/stressed-nation-74-uk-overwhelmed-or-unable-cope-some-point-past-year.

5. At this point you may be wondering why I didn't include tolerance in my list of good fruits. Tolerance is indeed a good thing, but not in the way that it has been so often applied in the Postmodern thought. Tolerance is seen as an absolute and if you hold any sort of conviction, you are intolerant of other beliefs. This is a toxic mindset. In a speech given at Biola University by esteemed apologist Josh McDowell, he points out the shift in the use of tolerance as we use it today. He said that "tolerance used to mean putting up with someone who is intolerable" but now means "all values and truth claims are equally valid". This kind of tolerance is not a good thing in my opinion because it limits our ability to call out and fix bad ideas in our society.

6. Krakauer, Jon, and David Vann. *Into the Wild.* London: Picador, 2018.

7. "Postmodern Nonsense Meets Palpable Evil." Desiring God, June 21, 2020. https://www.desiringgod.org/interviews/postmodern-nonsense-meets-palpable-evil.

8. Courtois, Stephane. *Black Book of Communism: Crimes, Terror, Repression*. Place of publication not identified: Harvard Univ Press, 2015.

9. Bird, Brad. *The Incredibles*. USA: Disney, 2005.

Chapter 8: The Soil of Polarization

1. "Who Joins Cults?" Education Week, February 25, 2019. https://www.edweek.org/ew/articles/1982/11/03/02120011.h02.html.

2. If you still think that "being silent is violent" and contributes to the problem, then I would encourage you to read this article by Samuel Sey titled "If silence is violence, Jesus is a sinner". While we should care about social justice, silence does not imply compliance as observed from the life of Jesus. Sey, Samuel. "If Silence Is Violence, Jesus Is A Sinner." Slow To Write, June 14, 2020. https://slowtowrite.com/if-silence-is-violence-jesus-is-a-sinner/.

3. I don't think you could find a sane person on the right or the left that doesn't think racism or systemic racism is evil. The question is not "is systemic racism evil" that has America divided, but "does systemic racism exist". I believe that once we understand these distinctions, we will be able to have better, more civil conversations about these issues without assuming the other person to be a racist for disagreeing.

4. In regard to my opinion on the whole Church opening scenario, I am fully supportive of their reasoning and motivation in defying orders. John MacArthur put it best in his message addressing the reasoning, so I suggest you go read that as well, but I will spill out a few of my thoughts. The fact that the governor deemed Planned Parenthood clinics and marijuana dispensaries "essential" and neglected to put the Church in that category is outrageous and an attack against the Church and religion. I think that shutting down the very institution that gives so many people hope and meaning in their life has left them to search for meaning elsewhere whether it be in vigorous

political participation or dangerous riots. I think that the salvation of souls is something that is not only essential but is the ultimate goal of our lives here on earth.

Chapter 9: The Problem at the Roots

1. Solzhenitsyn, Aleksandr. *The Gulag Archipelago*. Vintage Publishing, 2018.

2. Solzhenitsyn Aleksandr Isaevich. *A World Split Apart*. McLean, VA: Trinity Forum, 2002.

3. Augustine, and Peter Constantine. *Confessions*. New York, NY: W. W. Norton & Company, 2020.

4. Edwards, Jonathan. *God Glorified in Man's Dependence*. Paradise Valley, AZ: Camelback Bible Church, 1998.

5. 1 Corinthians 9:23

6. Jorge Gabriel Rodriguez Reyes January 26, and Nancy Brown January 27. "What's Wrong with the World?" Society of Gilbert Keith Chesterton, November 16, 2018. https://www.chesterton.org/wrong-with-world/

Chapter 10: Healing the Roots

1. Williams Thaddeus J. *Reflect: Becoming Yourself by Mirroring the Greatest Person in History.* Wooster, OH: Weaver Book Company, 2017.

2. Lewis, C. S. *The Abolition of Man.* Place of publication not identified: Exciting Classics, 2013.

3. Nietzsche, Friedrich Wilhelm. *The Will to Power.* London: Allen, 1924.